IV

Careers Behind
the Screen

TV

Careers Behind the Screen

JANE BLANKSTEEN
AVI ODENI

John Wiley & Sons, Inc.
New York • Chichester • Brisbane • Toronto • Singapore

This publication is designed to provide accurate and authoritative information in
regard to the subject matter covered. It is sold with the understanding that the
publisher is not engaged in rendering professional advice. If professional advice
or other expert assistance is required, the services of a competent professional
person should be sought.

Blanksteen, Jane.
   TV, careers behind the screen.

   Bibliography: p.
   1. Television—Production and direction—Vocational
guidance.   2. Television authorship—Vocational
guidance.   3. Television graphics—Vocational guidance.
I. Odeni, Avi.   II. Title.
PN1992.75.B53 1987   791.45'023'023   86-24713
ISBN 0-471-84815-8

Printed in the United States of America

87 88 10 9 8 7 6 5 4 3 2 1

To Flo
For Her
Neverending Laughter

Contents

Foreword

The proliferation of university-level degree programs in television over the past 20 years is evidence of the increasing number of people who are interested in becoming professionals in the television industry. A generation has grown up on television and, for better or worse, they now want to be a part of the action—not just consumers of it.

Those of us who teach and administer these university programs are regularly faced with the ubiquitous question—"Are there jobs in the industry?" I often envy my colleagues in less creatively oriented academic disciplines who either have a ready positive response or don't have to face the question at all.

I've developed a stock response which goes something like, "Yes, there are jobs for those people with both the dedication and the talent." This answer could serve for any human endeavor, but there is really no other way to characterize the situation. While there is no sure-fire recipe for a successful career in television, *TV: Careers Behind the Screen* provides a clear, concise, honest explanation of the important factors which bear on how one finds work in the field.

This book provides a well-organized, up-to-date description of the organization of the television industry—no mean task. Once consisting mainly of local television stations and networks, the industry is now a multi-tiered complex of broadcast stations; national, regional, cable, and syndicated networks; advertising agencies; production houses; community access cable outlets; and private and public institutional media centers. This book incorporates a comprehensive understanding of the recent changes in television industry opportunities, noting the important technological innovations, such as satellite distribution, miniaturization of equipment, computerized editing systems—all of which have had a dramatic effect on the changing job market.

TV: Careers Behind the Screen has limited its objectives to a specific segment of the television industry—those jobs relating to the production of television programs. The information in this book may serve to whet the appetite of a student surveying possible career alternatives, but the book is primarily for people who have already been bitten by the bug, either through personal production experience or actual professional experience. It lays out, in logical order, the jobs, how to go about getting them, and finally, candid interviews with a cross section of people actually working in television production.

The selection of interviewees is especially helpful since it represents various samples of people doing ostensibly the same job in very different production organizations. We hear, for instance, from a sound man at a local cable access channel describing his job and how he got it, followed by a sound man at a large production house in New York City. There's no attempt to imply that one job is any better than the other, but the pros and cons of each are instructive.

Working in a small market may provide a fulfilling career for the person with the right temperament. There is open discussion about the continuing dilemma facing people interested in working in production: "Do I need a college degree? Should I major in 'communications'?"

This problem relates to the age old conundrum: You've got to have experience to get the job, but you can't get experience if you haven't had a job. Increasingly, university programs in television have redesigned curricula to develop meaningful courses of study in film/television education. At various times programs have erred at both extremes, producing graduates with either a great deal of experience with too little liberal arts background to function effectively in television's world of

ideas, or a concentrated liberal arts curriculum with virtually
no emphasis on practical entry-level production skills. Currently, many college and university communications programs
offer a balance of liberal arts coursework and sufficient production opportunities for students to demonstrate their potential talent.

Various jobs are defined, and the specific kind of training
required for each job is discussed. The authors make no attempt to imply that there is only one way to prepare for any
specific job. The television industry isn't that categorical. But
my experience bears out the authors' research which provides
a dependable list of indicators for each job description.

This book addresses the most contemporary development in
television production: the increasing overlapping of film and
video in feature film production and distribution. There has
been a dramatic increase in crossover training by cinematog-
raphers, film editors, and production personnel. Universities,
unions, networks, and production companies have recognized
this trend and have responded with programs to prepare for
the inevitable industry impact. At New York University, we
have begun cross-training all undergraduate students in both
film and video in response to the current professional needs.

This book cannot, of course, serve as a personal contact
with someone in the television business. But, reflective of the
kind of practical advice it provides, the authors remind job
seekers to develop any and all personal contacts with people
in the industry—whether direct or indirect. The information
here is fresh, knowledgeable, and useful. This book should be
in the library of anyone seriously interested in pursuing a
career in television production.

LAWRENCE J. LUNDINO
Head of Undergraduate Studies
Department of Film and Television
New York University

How to Use This Book

TV: Careers Behind the Screen is a practical who-what-where-why guide to behind-the-scenes television production jobs in everything from the networks to the burgeoning field of corporate and industrial nonbroadcast television. It is your hands-on guide to understanding what production crew members, producers, directors, writers, engineers, videotape editors, and graphic artists actually do.

Reading this book is like having a relative in the television production business—someone who can tell you what it's really like to work behind the screen . . . and how to get there. We will take you where we went: into the offices, labs, newsrooms, edit rooms, and studios of network, local, cable, and private television. Graphic artists, writers, directors, producers, technicians, engineers, videotape editors, camera operators, and even high level executives tell what their jobs *really* entail, what they like and dislike about their work, what skills you need, how you can break into the business, what really should be in your resume, and how you can find the right person to get you started.

While *TV: Careers Behind the Screen* covers a host of jobs in television production, it does not cover on-camera careers—the actors, reporters, announcers, hosts, and anchors you see on the screen. There are other books on the market that deal with those "glamour" jobs. Managerial, sales, legal, public relations, marketing, advertising, administrative, computer communications, and other careers—essential parts of the television business—are also not the concern of this book. As Grant A. Tinker says in an interview in this book, such jobs "are really no different than they are at General Foods or Procter and Gamble. The only difference is that instead of getting soap into stores, we're getting entertainment programming to television stations . . ."

We've organized the book's chapters according to the basic types of production skills: the production crew, writers, producers, directors, videotape editors, engineers, and graphic artists. Each chapter is designed to stand as an independent unit outlining the role each job plays in television production, career paths within that line of work, job hunting tips, advice about education and training, information on future trends that could affect that profession. *A Day With* . . . sections walk you through an actual day's work and *A Talk With* . . . sections let you hear what professionals have to say about their work.

In the back of the book you will find additional useful information: pay scales in different areas of television production, lists of associations that can help you in your career, and schools providing training.

We urge you to read not only "your" chapter, but the others as well. Television is a team effort. Whether you are aiming for a career as an engineer or producer, it is important to understand what other people contribute to getting a show on the air. The more you know about it, the better prepared you will be to get your first job, and do it well.

That's not the only reason to read the whole book. Many chapters are interrelated. Jobs overlap; writers often become producers and directors. Engineers, videotape editors, and production crew members should know each other's jobs; the lines between them aren't that rigid. Graphic arts jobs and videotape editing are merging; there is a growing number of artist/engineering positions.

No matter what kind of television production career you are interested in, be sure to read the first two chapters. "What Is Television?" gives you background on the industry, the programming and the employers. "How to begin Your Television Production Career" provides useful information about how to get a job and important details about foot-in-the-door entry-level jobs.

Just as teamwork is a vital part of daily life in television production, so it was in the making of this book. We could not have written this book without the generosity of many professionals at the networks, stations, studios, and corporations across the country who opened their doors and studios to us, and answered our questions fully and candidly. Our informants' eagerness to share their information is a direct reflection of their excitement and love for the television medium. On behalf of anyone who has ever wondered about what it's like behind the screen, we thank them for telling us the way it really is and how to get there.

THANKS

Many, many thanks to the following people for sharing with us and helping us to write this book:

Francine Achbar	Kirk Daniels
Tom Appleby	Norm Davidson
Steve Aveson	Jack Davis
Jerry Berger	Richard Lee Dickinson
Joe Berini	Timothy Dwight
David Blanksteen	Ralph Famiglietta, Jr.
Deborah Boldt	Angela Fernan
Mia Drake Brandt	Jay Fine
Gary Brasher	Carmen Finestra
Peggy Brim	Jill Flegenheimer
Bob Brooks	Lawrence Fraiberg
Electa Brown	Reuven Frank
Douglas Brush	Bob Franklin
Ted Bruss	Mark R. Fratrik
Red Burns	Cindy Fraust
Tab Butler	Catherine Gay
Kevin Cheslack-Postava	Steve Giangrasso
Sue Cohen	Joe Gianquinto
Hal Cooper	Margorie Thue Gil
Robert Cornet	Arnold Giordano

William Goldman
Cheryl Gould
Peter Grad
Merrill Grant
Lawrence Grossman
Brad Hagen
Kevin Hale
Iona Harper
Martha Harris
Jane Hartley
Biff Henderson
Ed Hobson
Sheldon Hoffman
Tom Hyre
Janice Kaplan
Alex Kariacou
Doris Katz
James A. Kaye
Jo Lauria
Bobby Lee Lawrence
Allan Leicht
Louis Libin
Beverly Littlewood
Aimee Liu
Tom Madaras
Lynn Malmud
Steve Marchand
Charles Marcus
Ann McGruddy
Katie McGuire
Stephen C. Mulligan

Andy Nelson
Marylou O'Callahan
Judy O'Sullivan
James Owens
Billy Pittard
Pat Quarles
Joe Raznik
Missie Rennie
Peter Restivo
Harold Reynolds
Antonio Richardson
Mary E. Rothschild
M. S. Rukeyser
David Salant
Katherine Scaccia
Debbie Schmidt
Judy Seabridge
Leon Sirulnik
Elan Soltes
Roger Stauss
Marie Stroud
Eleanor Timberman
Grant A. Tinker
George Thompson
Peter Tomic
Bill Topazio
Fabio Toscano
Judy Tygard
Inga Van Der Sluis
Al Wasser

Thanks also to American Film Institute, Center for Communication, Inc., Directors Guild of America, Grass Valley Group, International Television Association, National Broadcasting Company, NBC News, The National Association of Broadcasters, New York University's Tisch School of the Arts, Television Information Office, and The Writers Guild of America, East.

This book is dedicated to the loving memory of Miriam Odeni.

JANE BLANKSTEEN AND AVI ODENI

1

What Is Television?

This chapter introduces you to television programming and production in a way that will help prepare you to enter the television job market better informed about the business.

For our purposes, television means the production and airing of television programs. In business terms, the television industry is the business of making a product (programs) and persuading people to "buy" the product (watch the programs). When you subscribe to premium service television such as a movie channel, or buy or rent a videocassette, you are more literally purchasing the product. In traditional parlance, however, "sales" in television terms means viewership.

Television programs reach the public through the three major networks and their affiliates, and through local, public, independent, and superstations. There are also several cable networks and specialized cable channels for sports, sex, religious, and other programming. You can pay extra for premium cable services like Home Box Office and Cinemax, or for one-shot important sports and entertainment events through pay-per-view television. Original video entertainment and various instructional programs are now available on videocassette along with the more familiar taped motion pictures.

If you are interested in a career in television, you should become familiar with all these branches of the industry, how they differ, and what a career in each can mean.

TELEVISION JOB OPPORTUNITIES

There are over 1,200 broadcast television stations in the United States. Of these, more than 600 are network affiliates, about 300 are noncommercial public television, and about 300 are independent stations.

Cable television—"narrowcast" stations—bring additional programming to subscribers whose homes are wired to cable systems in their geographical area.

Corporate or private television is nonbroadcast television programming that is used to inform employees (salesforce, management, etc.) about different aspects of the business. While it may be a relatively small segment of the industry and less glamorous than the networks, private television is growing and becoming an important source of jobs.

Whether broadcast or cable, television stations can be highly profitable business investments. In 1984, commercial television received $19.0 billion in advertising revenues.

The three major networks—ABC, CBS, and NBC—own 14 of the larger stations in the country. Corporations such as Cox Communications, Warner Amex, Time Inc. and Westinghouse own many stations. Several stations owned by one parent company are called *group-owned* stations. Group W is one such group, owned by Westinghouse Broadcasting and Cable Inc.

In cable, a company that owns several cable systems is known as a *multiple system operator* or MSO. More than 50 percent of all television stations are group owned; the majority of cable stations are owned by MSOs.

A surprising number of corporations have their own departments that produce private television programming for their own use. In 1985, there were approximately 8,500 such organizations according to Douglas Brush, a partner of D/J Brush Associates, a management consulting firm specializing in corporate communications issues.

Networks

A *network* is a centralized source of programming. There are several kinds of networks: broadcast, cable, independent, public television, ad hoc, cooperative, and private television.

The three major networks—ABC, CBS, and NBC—are not television stations. Rather their business is producing television programming and selling advertisers the opportunity to advertise on these programs.

The advertising rates a network can charge are determined by how many people watch the network's programming. Accordingly, it is in any network's best interest to get as large an audience as possible—the larger the audience, the higher the advertising rates. Therefore, a network's priority is getting the show aired on as many stations as possible.

The networks have two main outlets for their programming: their *owned-and-operated* stations (O&O) and their affiliates. The three major networks own and operate a total of 14 stations. O&Os, which are in major markets such as Los Angeles and New York, have such large viewership that they can set programming trends. Each of the top three O&Os reaches about 19 percent of U.S. households with television sets.

The rest of the stations that air the network's programming are *affiliates*, stations that agree to air a certain portion of the network's programming at certain hours and share the local advertising revenues. In 1985, ABC had 215 affiliate stations, CBS had 204, and NBC had 207. About 65 percent of an affiliate's programming is network-supplied, via satellite or microwave, at specific times. Of the remainder, about 15 percent is produced locally by the affiliate station, and 20 percent is syndicated programming such as movies, reruns, game shows, and the like.

In public television, the network system is almost the opposite of the network-affiliate system. The Public Broadcasting Service (PBS) supplies basic programming to its *member stations*. Member stations pay dues to PBS and also pay for the programming they choose to use.

A *cable television network* offers a package of programming to a cable system. It might be 24-hour news or weather coverage and is paid by the cable system on a per-subscriber basis.

When an independent station, one not affiliated with the three broadcast networks, produces programming for distribution to other independent stations, you have an *independent network*. For example, New York City's WPIX, an independent, now offers Independent Network News, which is distributed nationwide in the same way as a major network's news program.

An *ad hoc network* is a consortium of independent stations and some affiliates who join together to air first-run programming during prime time. Sometimes an advertiser will create the network—as Mobil Corporation did to produce the Royal Shakespeare Company's production of Nicholas Nickleby. Program producers, such as Metromedia, Embassy, and Paramount, sometimes form ad hoc networks.

Private television networks are a relatively recent phenomenon. They are usually a centrally located television production studio that produces programming shown on television monitors at various corporate locations. Some corporate television networks provide live airings of programming, others transmit via satellite and other methods to branch offices around the country. At its most primitive, videocassettes are distributed by mail to offices equipped with videotape players.

Independent Stations

Independent stations are not affiliated with any network and must supply all of their own programming. They produce their own shows (such as local news and public affairs) and may pick up from sources like Independent Network News, syndicated programs, movies, and reruns.

Superstations

A *superstation* is an independent television station whose signal is delivered nationally by many cable systems. The first superstation was WTBS (Turner Broadcasting Systems) created by Ted Turner, head of the Cable News Network (CNN). Superstations, which include WGN in Chicago, and WOR in New York, produce a variety of programming including news, documentaries, public affairs shows, and in-depth news series. In addition, they offer programming produced by others such as movies, live sports, reruns of former network programs (off network series), and syndicated programming.

Cable Television

Originally developed to bring television signals to remote communities, *cable television* currently delivers programming to an estimated 34.1 million subscribers nationwide—more than 40 percent of America's television households, according to A. C. Nielsen. Paul Kagan Associates, Inc., an industry observer, predicts that by 1990, the total number of households hooked up to cable should grow to an estimated 56.8 million.

To fulfill FCC regulations that a cable system provide community-oriented shows in exchange for the right to wire an area, cable television systems also produce local news, community affairs, and talk shows.

Much local cable programming is quite simple and low-budget making smaller cable stations an ideal place to get your first job in television. However, in larger cable markets some shows are approaching network quality which means that, like local broadcast stations, they may not be willing to train many inexperienced people. (Ironically, the larger and more profitable stations are least willing to train newcomers. Programs with high ratings are so valuable that producers are reluctant to take any chances with inexperienced staff who could bungle a show.)

Private Television or Corporate Communication

Corporations of all kinds are producing their own *private television* programs. Their facilities range from small departments with one staff producer to network quality studios with large full-time staffs of television professionals. Some private television departments offer services to other corporations that have found the medium ideal for bringing information to employees in widely scattered locations and for training their salesforce and other personnel.

Since Americans have come to expect network-quality production when they watch TV, corporate television programming must be well-produced if it is to be effective. As a result, private television is now attracting experienced network and cable professionals by offering competitive salaries, more normal hours, and a growing commitment to quality.

Home Video ————————————————————————

With the popularity of the VCR in the 1980s, programming produced specifically for homes, schools, and businesses has become increasingly important. In 1985, there were approximately 40,111 video titles available to consumers, schools, corporations, and healthcare facilities. More than 32 percent of those video titles are in the general interest/education category, 23 percent are health/science, 21 percent are movies/entertainment, and an estimated 18 percent of the titles are accompanied by workbooks or other supplementary materials.

THE PRODUCERS OF PROGRAMMING ————————

The three major networks each provide about 22 hours of programming for prime time (8 PM to 11 PM, Monday through Saturday; 7 PM to 11 PM on Sunday) each week, or 3,432 hours a year. With such a demand for programming, it is not surprising that television offers a gamut of everything and anything.

Most series produce 26 weeks worth of programming each year and rerun these shows the remainder of the year—usually in the spring and summer. Off network series are a different kind of reruns: old programs that have generated at least 130 shows and can therefore provide a 26-week, 5-days-a-week schedule, are sold to independent and local stations.

The majority of programming is produced by independent production companies. For example, *Donahue,* the show hosted by Phil Donahue, is carried on the local NBC station in New York City and on an ABC affiliate in Philadelphia. *Donahue* is a syndicated show produced by Multimedia, a major independent production company that sells its programs to stations around the country, whether affiliates of any or all of the three major networks, or independent stations. *Dallas,* on the other hand is a CBS program, but while it is commissioned by CBS, it too is produced by an independent production company. In fact, in 1986, only three prime-time entertainment shows, NBC's *Punky Brewster,* CBS's *Twilight Zone,* and ABC's *Moonlighting* were produced in-house by the networks.

Networks do produce some of their own programming—mostly news, public affairs, and talk shows. Antitrust laws limit broadcast networks in the amount of in-house prime-time programming they may produce.

The three networks all produce their own two-hour morning news/entertainment programs, evening news programs, and public affairs shows, documentaries, specials, election, inaugural, and international summit coverage—all for distribution to their owned-and-operated and affiliate stations.

Local stations, whether affiliate or independent, generally produce some of their own programming.

Cable networks provide the bulk of a cable station's programming, with less than 1 percent of programming produced locally. Local production is usually confined to news and community affairs.

The programs produced by nonbroadcast private (corporate) television are less varied: they include training programs, employee pep talks, corporate news, and teleconferences between staff members at various locations.

How Network-Commissioned Programs Are Produced

Network-commissioned programs, such as *Dallas, The A-Team,* and *Kate & Allie,* begin as ideas offered by independent production firms. Network programmers, headed by a director of programming, sift through thousands of initial proposals each year, of which less than two dozen become programs on the air.

The program production process works something like this:

1. Independent producers provide concepts to a network.
2. The network commissions a *treatment*—an outline of the proposed series, descriptions of the principal characters, their relationships and ideas for how, in the case of a soap opera, the drama might unfold.

3. If the network likes the treatment, it asks the producers to develop the proposed program further. The network pays the producers "development dollars" and commissions more scripts. In exchange for the development dollars, the network gets creative control over the program and first refusal rights for scripts.
4. The network begins choosing actors. (Generally, networks have their own casting directors.)
5. A sample, full-scale episode is produced for testing with audiences.

The High-Risk Economics of Producing

Production companies who produce series for the networks actually lease the programs to the networks. In 1986, production (and film) companies spent as much as $1.6 million per episode, typically losing between $300,000 and $500,000 per episode.

So, where's the pay-off? In off network syndication. Syndication rights for a series can sell for as much as $200 million for five years. CBS's *Magnum, P.I.* brought its producers approximately $1.8 million per episode in syndication. The price for NBC's *The Cosby Show*'s eventual syndication rights is estimated at $2 million per episode.

If syndication sale prices sound extraordinarily high, consider the risks the production companies took initially. Also consider the fact that in order to qualify for syndication, in which a show airs five times a week, a show must have at least five seasons worth of programming. In other words, the show has to have been a big success—and in television, success doesn't come easily.

As a television job hunter, you need to know the basic economics of the system. Profits depend on audience size which dictates how much an advertiser will pay for airtime. Producers of programming with the biggest audiences tend to have more money for production and salaries, which in turn often leads to higher quality programs.

How does this affect you? The more advertising dollars there are at stake, the less likely are the producers to take a

chance on beginners. The conventional wisdom is that you
start in a smaller market—one with a smaller audience. As
you gain experience you can move up to a larger market. The
"big time," or "major leagues," is network programming, which
commands the largest audience share of all. Bear in mind,
though, that working on network programming doesn't necessarily mean being employed by a network. It could mean being employed by a Hollywood entertainment studio that is
supplying the network with its programs.

A Talk With . . .

Grant A. Tinker
*Former Chairman of the Board and Chief Executive Officer,
NBC*

> *Grant A. Tinker has worked for NBC three times since
> 1949 when he joined the company as a management
> trainee. Before rejoining NBC for the third time in 1981,
> Tinker had been president of MTM Enterprises which
> produced such shows as* The Mary Tyler Moore Show,
> The Bob Newhart Show, Phyllis, Rhoda, WKRP in
> Cincinnati, *and* Lou Grant. *During his tenure at MTM,
> the company's shows won more than two dozen Emmys
> as well as numerous other awards.*

Right out of college I wanted to get into publishing but publishing had no interest in me. So, I came to 30 Rockefeller
Plaza [NBC's New York City headquarters] and knocked on
the door of the personnel department, not knowing very
much about the broadcasting business and certainly not
having any burning desire to be in it. All I had was a radio
listener's awareness of the medium—it was 1949 and television was not a factor at the time. I got an entry-level job here
at NBC, for a while, working nights and weekends in radio
operations.

I didn't actually get into television until 1954 when I got a
catch-all job with a personal manager who represented several performers like Bob and Ray. We also produced some
local afternoon television shows at WPIX, WABC, and WNBC

here in New York. So, you could say I got into television from the production end of it.

No Complaints

When I began, I certainly wasn't sure that television was the right place for me. But one thing I can say is that it always has been interesting and consuming. I've never had a job in television that wasn't—and I've had a variety of them.

I really have no complaints about working in television. As long as you have to work for a living, it's as good a place to work as any. Television is interesting, it's topical, and it's constantly with you. It's as present as your television set so that you're never without your business. I like that it's a 24-hour matter. On occasion it may bother my wife, my children, and friends that I'm involved and connected to my work all the time. But it doesn't bother me. Almost as far back as I can remember, I have considered my work as a seven days a week matter . . .

Another thing I like about television is working with creative people—especially writers. I am a great admirer of those who have both the talent and discipline to produce good writing. To write for a television series is a relentless job. You no sooner have one script done and it's into production than you have to get into the next one.

Sometimes I feel a twinge of jealousy for those who are in the creative process. I'm not a writer, but had I tried writing and applied myself I'm not sure I couldn't have been a good writer. But since I don't really know whether I could have done it, I'm content to rub elbows with creative people who do.

Advice

Most people looking for jobs in television have to expect disappointment and closed doors in the beginning. Television is a pretty closed business. People in it may move around and change jobs a lot, but they're the same people moving around within the universe of television. It's hard for an outsider to get from the outside in, but obviously it can be done—because here we all are. We all got in somehow.

My advice, then, is don't get discouraged. Television is such a worthwhile way to make a living and spend your day—that's why it's so very popular. Those who persevere will eventually get through the door. I know that's true, because, as I said, here we all are. There is, however, one thing you can do, and it's true for job hunting in any business: Cultivate, wherever you can, relationships with people who are already in the business. If they don't have jobs for you, they may know people who do . . .

As for education, I think liberal arts is a better choice than communications. There is a great deal more attention paid to communications in schools than there is room in the business for all those communications graduates. While you might minor in communications, I see a liberal arts major as a kind of insurance. To come out of school with a communications major and then not be able to use it would be a waste of the college opportunity.

The Easiest and the Hardest Way

Unless you have a specific skill in television production, being a writer is in a sense the easiest—yet the hardest—way to begin. As a writer, you can sit down at home alone and write. You don't need access to special equipment to produce evidence of your abilities. Of course, the hard part is getting someone to read what you've written, and to make judgments about it. But there is conceivably more opportunity for good writers because good writers are the hardest people to find.

People should also remember that working for a network isn't the only way to work in television. There are only three networks and almost 1,000 stations in the country, about 600 of which are network affiliates, with the remainder independents. The majority of people working in broadcasting wind up at stations, not the networks. Working at individual stations is a very good way to make a living. It's not only a good way to start a career, but a good way to end one. It may be even better than working for a network.

The Future of Television

I don't think the nature of broadcasting will change with large corporations buying television networks. A corporation has to look at broadcasting as an island within the company. The television business is not like other businesses—we live by different rules, we operate differently. The heads of those

corporations understand that they cannot and should not su-
perimpose their methods of management on us . . .

Right now, networks are limited in the amount of prime-time
entertainment programming we can produce ourselves, though
we are allowed to produce our own news and sports. Those
laws are probably going to change in the 1990s, but I think even
then the networks shouldn't try to attract and employ all the
creative people themselves. I think it's good when we have a
variety of sources from which we can select and buy our programming. I think that way we tend to get better programs . . .

The news and sports divisions are more my idea of broadcasting anyway. Entertainment programming is a very different
business—it's the entertainment business. Accordingly, we buy
our television movies, dramatic series and situation comedies
from places like Twentieth Century Fox and Universal.

As broadcasters, all we do is choose when and where to air
the entertainment programs. After that, it becomes a matter
for the engineering people to get it on the air and the sales
people selling time to advertisers. The marketing and sales
jobs are really no different than they are at General Foods or
Procter and Gamble. The only difference is that instead of
getting soap into stores, we're getting entertainment programming to television stations . . .

As for advances in technology, I think they will only bring new
opportunities for creative people because they have brought
more players into the game. Now, in addition to the networks
as major markets for programming, there are the various cable companies, superstations and an entire new market in
original video cassettes. This gives writers, producers and
production people more markets for their work.

A Talk With . . .

Lawrence K. Grossman
President, NBC News

> *Larry Grossman has played a significant role in both com-
> mercial and public television news and public affairs pro-
> gramming. Before becoming president of NBC News in
> 1984, Larry was president and chief executive officer of*

the Public Broadcasting Service for eight years, during which time he helped originate shows including the PBS series Vietnam: A Television History, Frontline, *and* Inside Story. *It was also during his tenure that* The Mac-Neil/Lehrer Report *expanded to a one-hour format.*

Since Grossman joined NBC News as its President, more people now watch NBC News' daily broadcasts than any other network's. Among the programming projects Grossman has spearheaded is "The New Cold War," an unprecedented division-wide effort designed to examine the state of Soviet-American relations, and Main Street, *a breakthrough new television series for children.*

When I came to New York in 1953, I wanted to work as a writer in the magazine business. But, after months of pounding the pavement, I was rejected by almost every magazine thinkable. I did, however, get a job at *Look* magazine in their promotion department as a promotion writer. It was a way to get my foot in the door. Part of my job became seeking publicity for *Look* articles through television. We tried to get the articles featured on programs such as *Today* and *The Ed Sullivan Show . . .* Through that, I met people in television and by 1955 it became clear to me that TV was a growing, exciting field and that I wanted to explore it some more. So, I wrote a letter to the head of advertising at CBS and, fortunately, a job for a copywriter opened up.

In 1962, I left CBS and went to NBC where I was in charge of advertising and worked a lot with the news department. Then I left NBC to found my own company—an advertising and production company specializing in public affairs. My television clients included NBC, CBS, Teleprompter and WNET/New York, Children's Television Workshop (CTW), and PBS.

180 Degree Turn

Later, when PBS was looking for their second president, they asked me. At first I turned them down. But then, I went home to my wife and she asked why. I said I had my own company and we were doing very well, I had commitments to my employees, I had commitments to clients. And, besides, I'd decided never to go back to working for a big organization again.

Then my wife said something that made my mind turn 180 degrees: "All your life you've been concerned about the quality of television, and you've been complaining that television is not as good as it could be. Here somebody is giving you the opportunity to take a job where you can really have some influence, and you're turning it down for all kinds of reasons, including that it's not enough money." Of course, she was right, and I ended up accepting the job.

Eight years later, Grant Tinker called and asked me to run NBC News. It was an unpredictable choice and an odd one. But, the job was something I'd always dreamed of. And, while it was painful to leave PBS, because I was very happy there, the NBC offer was irresistible.

Public vs. Commercial TV

Running PBS has been very different from NBC. While both are networks of stations, you don't actually produce anything at PBS. Rather, you stimulate production and develop ideas for programs. Other people then make the programs and you try to get money for them. PBS is purely public service and is a very important part of the communications spectrum.

Working for NBC News is very different, primarily because we produce our programs right here and are responsible for three hours of live programming every day. News is a business that is always changing, and so you have many crises and important decisions that have to be made quickly.

Being involved with the news is an important public service. You have a sense that you are doing something that's worth doing, that is useful to people, and helpful to our democracy. You're working with interesting and intelligent people. And the work itself is unpredictable—new things are always happening, new decisions have to be made and new ways of doing things have to be grappled with.

Also, you have to be concerned about being fair, being clear about what's happening in very complicated events and to do it all, often with very little preparation time. You also have an awesome responsibility in terms of dealing with sensitive news and information that could harm the national security. It is our job to make responsible decisions even if they may be controversial and unpopular.

Leaner Budgets in Both Public and Commercial TV

While public television depends on grants and commercial television depends on earnings, both of them involve working within a budget. And, though the budgets in commercial television may be larger, the process is really the same. I used to tell the people at PBS when they looked at commercial television and saw how much more financial resources there were, that even though the commercial budgets were a lot bigger, they never seem large enough to the people who have to administer them.

Right now there are government spending cutbacks which are affecting PBS. In commercial television, there is a similar problem. The television business used to be constantly growing and expanding. People were buying more television sets, and the population was increasing, so increased spending by broadcasters could always be quickly offset by increased advertising revenues. Now, however, we're in a period when the revenues are reaching a plateau. NBC is doing very well because we are getting a bigger share of the audience. But the total audience isn't growing dramatically. We're doing well because we're taking audience share away from others. But if we fall behind, we'll have financial problems, too.

Advice

Both public and commercial television are very hard to break into, largely because so many people want to get into them. The competition is fierce and there are not that many jobs open. Now that both public and commercial television have reached maturity, there is less opportunity for new people than there had been in the past.

Nonetheless, people with determination and patience can break in. I don't think there is any mystery or any secrets or short cuts. Luck is very important. So is persistence. When I was growing up in Brooklyn, every Sunday, Mayor Fiorello LaGuardia used to end his radio broadcast on WNYC with the phrase: "patience and fortitude." That's a very good guideline. You must be prepared to accept disappointment, but if you work hard and are persistent, chances are you can break in. I guess I am proof of that—I had no special contacts when I began, and it took me more than 20 years to get on the editorial side.

A Talk With . . .

Stephen C. Mulligan
Director of Audio Visual Communications,
Allstate Insurance Company; and
Former President, International Television Association (ITVA)

> *At Allstate Insurance Company in Northbrook, Illinois,*
> *Mulligan manages a staff of 30 video professionals. The*
> *department produces communications, motivational and*
> *training videotape programs for the insurance company's*
> *employees. It has won awards that include ITVA Gold*
> *and Silver Reels and U.S. Industrial Film Festival Cine*
> *Golden Eagles. In 1986 it produced 160 programs. Mulli-*
> *gan was president of the ITVA, the organization repre-*
> *senting nonbroadcast television people, from 1984 to*
> *1986 and is chairperson of IABC (International Associa-*
> *tion of Business Communicators) Electronics Communi-*
> *cations Council.*

My first job in television was as an intern with NBC. I'd won a
writing contest sponsored by my high school—my writing
sample was an interview with Shad Northshield who was
then producer of the Huntley-Brinkley Report. Shad submitted the interview to NBC's internship program, and I got an
internship with the Huntley–Brinkley Report during the 1968
national convention.

I thought I wanted to be in television until I had that internship. The work was kind of boring. It wasn't as glamorous as I
thought it would be. You just reported the news. It was so
routine—you just did the same thing day after day.

I ended up back in television through a back door. While I
was in school getting my MBA, I heard about a summer job as
a public relations writer at Allstate Insurance. I got that job
and gradually worked my way back into television by writing
a weekly TV news show. Eight years later I was managing the
video department staff and production studios.

Private Television Departments Nationwide

Private television is just starting to explode. According to the
Brush Report, there are about 8,000 private television departments nationwide today. Now that many corporations have

cut back layers of management, they are discovering that video can help spread limited management resources throughout the corporation. Also, there are a lot of changes in corporate life, and management has to explain what they are doing and why people should join in.

Video is an extremely powerful medium. If it's used right it can move mountains. The key is to get management to use it properly. Corporate TV has to be done right. You can't have just talking heads, because even though your audience will sit there, they will tune out. Corporate television has to be done professionally. It can't look like a home movie. If it's done poorly, the audience concentrates on the fact that it's amateurish and they lose the message.

Danger of Over-Using Video

As more corporations discover video, though, they should beware of the danger of abdicating communication to video. Video provides management with a tool. It provides a way of delivering a consistent message right down the line to all employees at different locations.

But management should also remain visible. Someone from management, for instance, should be there when a tape is shown. They should explain the purpose of the tape and have a discussion with the viewers.

Variety, Challenge and Opportunity

I enjoy corporate television because no two assignments are really the same. We get a lot of resumes from broadcasting professionals who are tired of editing the same shows. When you think about it, the jobs that are available in broadcasting can be boring. At a news show, you shoot the same people night after night in the studio. Or, if you manage to get assigned to the crew of "Dynasty"—which isn't easy—even that gets pretty formulaic.

But, in corporate television, every single show you do is a challenge. You're always working on a shoestring. You have to be creative. You have to sell your ideas and deal with corporate egos and politics. And, a subject like insurance can be really boring, so you have to be creative to make it interesting.

Also, in corporate television, you are a big frog in a little puddle. You are a resource to your company. You do a lot of problem solving every day. And, most private television departments are nonunion, so you end up doing a lot more things than you would in a union shop.

Advice

For a career in private television a business/communications degree would be ideal if it existed. Study communications, but take as many business courses as you are allowed to. If you have some business knowledge, you'll be able to communicate better with the client departments.

Internships are very helpful. It's important that you get experience in a corporate setting. While there is not a whole vast number of job openings—it seems like everyone and their puppy wants to get into corporate TV—but there are openings, and departments are expanding . . .

The ITVA is a great source of help to young people. Join and go to meetings at your local chapter. You'll meet people and they'll get to know your work. Also, they now have a job hotline for members. Employers who have job openings send information to the international office. We get all of our people from ITVA.

A Talk With . . .

Peter Grad
Executive Vice President of Creative Affairs, Twentieth Century Fox Television

Twentieth Century Fox Television, a division of Twentieth Century Fox, is a major producer of prime time entertainment programming for television. As executive vice president of Creative Affairs since 1979, Peter Grad oversees current programming and the development of new programming. Among the shows that he has been involved in are The Fall Guy, *which after five seasons on ABC is now going into syndication, and Mr. Belvedere which is in its third season on ABC. Three programs launched in the Fall of 1986 under Fox's supervision are: L.A. Law (NBC) which is produced by Steven Bochco the executive producer of* Hill Street Blues, The Wizard of Elm Street *(CBS), and* Cold Steel and Neon *for ABC.*

I always wanted to be in the entertainment business but I had been groomed for the business world. I went to the Wharton School of Business and became a partner in a Wall Street firm. The way I got into television is a little bit different from most. After working on Wall Street, I began producing theater for Broadway.

I got my first break in the television business when I developed an idea for a television series with Alan King. The show never did get produced, but I ended up getting a job with Paramount as their television liaison in New York. That was in 1977 when ABC, CBS and NBC still had their base in New York—now everybody is out here in California. But, back in 1977, Paramount had no one based in New York and Michael Eisner hired me to be the company's liaison in New York.

As an executive, I don't produce shows. I work for Twentieth Century Fox Television who hires producers, and I act as a middle man between our producers and the networks. There is no real training for executive jobs in television, but what I do has to do with how you deal with writers, how you deal with producers, and finally, your ability to sell those ideas to the networks.

Risky but with Rewards

To answer your next question, yes, now I'm doing what I always wanted to do. I always wanted to use whatever creative abilities I had to help create projects and work with writers and producers. What I like is that as an executive for a television entertainment company, I get a chance to use both my selling ability and my creative ability.

My most fun is with quality shows like *L.A. Law.* I like to see television producing programs like *St. Elsewhere, Cheers,* and *Hill Street Blues.* But, that doesn't mean you can't have action adventure shows like *The A Team* as well.

There are plenty of things not to like about working in television, but for me, those negatives are part of the nature of doing any business. Production costs are too high and network license fees are too low. Our risk is growing with the gap between what it costs us to produce a show and what the network gives us in license fees. That gap is getting wider, but the rewards are still there to be had.

Also, the cost of talent is very high, competition is fierce and getting fiercer. Studios like Twentieth Century Fox are suppliers. We supply programs to the network. We hire writers and producers to work for us and present the programs they create to the networks. But now more and more companies are getting into the television production business and so are the networks. The networks are now beginning to go directly to the talent. They are bypassing outside studios and snapping up a lot of the available talent to come in and write and produce for them exclusively.

Advice

Successful production people come from all different walks of life. There is no one way to learn or succeed. My advice, though, is to study literature. You should know as much about the classics as you can. There are only a certain number of stories, most of which are derived from the classics in one sense or another, so the more of a literary background you have the better off you are.

And of course, you need perseverance. Ninety percent of the response to the ideas and scripts we get from the outside is negative. You have to remember that it's a lot easier for people to say no to your ideas than to say yes.

You have to have a very strong feeling about what you're doing and why. What the successful creative people I know have in common is their own vision. It's not a vision that is a little bit of theirs, a little bit of the network's, and a little bit of the studio's. That vision is theirs. I think if the executives at the networks and studios had that special kind of creative vision—they'd be producers, not executives.

2

How to Begin Your TV Production Career

Several aspects of behind-the-screen work in television are the same no matter what career you choose. This chapter covers important general information about training, education, resumes, cover letters, and preparing for interviews.

Of course, there are requirements and guidelines that are specific to particular careers such as engineering or graphic design. You will find that information in the relevant chapters.

BE WILLING TO . . .

When it comes to getting a job that will lead to producing or directing, we offer these commandments: *be willing to*

1. start at the bottom and do it gracefully,
2. go anywhere in the country, no matter how far away, no matter how dinky the station or company,
3. work long and hard hours,
4. accept low pay for many years,
5. work for free and take an additional paying job if necessary,
6. work for a program that is not your first love and respect the program and its audience for what they are, and

7. change jobs often—not just positions, but also companies and stations—in order to progress.

It is no accident that all of the above commandments begin with the phrase: be willing to. Being willing (and not willful) is an essential characteristic when it comes to success in television. The necessity for teamwork, the pressure of tight deadlines, the high cost of mistakes and other pressures, make television production something akin to being part of an army. When you are starting out, consider yourself a private and behave accordingly: be ready and willing to work and when you work, give 100 percent of yourself.

KEEP YOURSELF INFORMED

There are several ways you can prepare yourself for a production job without anyone's help. We will discuss them next.

Read, Read, Read . . .

Before applying for a job in television production—even an entry-level job such as production assistant—make sure that you are well-informed about the basics of television production. If you can't learn from witnessing or participating in production, the next best thing is to *read* about it. Read about all aspects of production—lighting, switching, camera operation, video and audio technology.

Books we recommend include a basic textbook on television production such as *Television Production* by Alan Wurtzel (McGraw-Hill Book Company, 1983) which provides thorough information about production activities and requirements; *Understanding Television Production* by Frank Iezzi (Prentice-Hall, Inc., 1984), which offers specific information about the crew members and their equipment; *The Cool Fire* by Bob Shanks (Vintage Books, 1977), an anecdotal overview of production from the producer's and production staff's point of view.

Read magazines such as *Videography, Television Broadcast, Millimeter, Video Systems,* and *Broadcasting*. In addition to finding informative articles about video production, you will also find job listings in the back of many of these industry magazines. Job listings are important not just for providing you with a list of jobs, but for giving you information about what employers are looking for.

If you are interested in TV news, read newspapers and news magazines. If you are interested in entertainment television, read *Variety* and *Backstage.* For news about all kinds of television programming, read advertising trade papers such as *Advertising Age* and *Ad Week* which often have excellent articles about current television programming and new shows.

Watch, Watch, Watch . . .

The most informative source of information about television is television itself. The best way to learn about television is to watch, especially the kinds of shows you want to work for. In addition to educating your eyes and ears, you can also watch the credits for the names of independent production companies to which you might apply for work. You can also get the names of key production people from the credits.

In addition to watching current programs, make a point of seeing old programs that were successful. Some museums have video libraries. In New York City, The Museum of Broadcasting is devoted to television programming. The American Film Institute in Washington, D.C. is another good source of information about television programming. If you can't find a repository of old programs, watch reruns now in syndication on your own set. Reruns are programs that lasted for five years on the air, which means they were popular and sometimes good.

Join, Join, Join . . .

Join professional associations such as the Institute of Electrical and Electronics Engineers, Inc. (IEEE) (which, incidentally, offers student memberships and provides publications and services for students), International Radio and Television Society, National Academy of Television Arts and Sciences (NATA), The Society of Motion Picture and Television Engineers (SMPTE), and the International Television Association

(ITVA). There are also other organizations/associations geared towards specific markets such as crew members, writers, producers or directors, which you can find listed in the appendix.

These associations provide publications and other sources of information very useful to the production professional and student alike. Watch for notices of field trips and special lectures sponsored by the magazines and/or their organizations. Field trips to television studios, production houses, and manufacturers can be both important sources of information and contacts.

Contact Professional Unions

Unions representing television professionals are also excellent sources of information about careers, training, and even specific job openings. You will find the names of unions listed within appropriate chapters and in the Appendix.

TRAINING AND EDUCATION

The subject of training and education is a sore one for many television professionals. With the exception, perhaps, of engineers and certain technical work, there is no right school or right way to get training. Television production is not like law practice—there is no Harvard or Yale of television production.

When you are trying to determine what kind of education you ideally should have to pursue a career in television production, it is important that you examine your goals. You might want to specialize in one aspect of television production (lighting, cameras, writing, general crew work, producing . . .) or aim for a managerial position.

In general, a four-year college degree is always preferable, but is not necessary. If your career interest lies in a technical area, a two-year degree or high school education may be enough to get you your first job. Experience and knowledge of a specific area of production is key.

For producing or directing, a liberal arts degree and a

demonstrable general knowledge is most useful. For engineering positions, a BS in electrical engineering is important. For positions operating equipment, a communications degree can be useful.

What about Journalism School?

When it comes to television news, journalism school rather than "media studies" is a touchy subject. No doubt the journalism schools offer important and valuable training. However, many professionals—even those who come out of journalism schools—stress the importance of on-the-job training. "Journalism school is all very well and good," observes one major market news director. "But it's the year out in the field that you really need."

Many professionals recommend the same thing: get some print or radio journalism experience under your belt. Work for your school newspaper, try to get an internship at a local paper in your college area, be willing to go out into the hinterlands and work for a small-town paper during your summer vacations or for your first year out of school.

The advantages of this approach are two-fold: First, you will prove that you can write and understand news—both very important skills for any television news jobs you may pursue later. Second, you can then qualify for television news writing jobs which are excellent for getting into producing and directing. (See Chapter 5 Writers.)

For specific advice about education and training, read the interviews with professionals throughout this book under the heading "A talk with . . ."

GETTING EXPERIENCE

Internships, Vendor Schools, Vacation Relief

In television, there is often the Catch-22 of "you can't get a job until you get experience and you can't get experience until you get a job." But there are exceptions and ways to get around that catch:

School Experience

While at school, try to get any hands-on television experience you can. Join video or even radio clubs and take any relevant courses in communications including journalism.

Internships

Actively seek out internship opportunities through your school or college and if necessary through individual television stations or private television departments. Internships are unpaid positions in which you work in exchange for school credit. Often they turn into job opportunities during the summer and possibly when you graduate.

1986 Internships, a book published by Writer's Digest Books has a list of internships you can apply for. Your school career advisory or television/radio/communications department may also have internship information. If you find no internship program, take the initiative to invent one.

If you are already a college graduate, and have no television experience, try for volunteer work at small stations (especially cable or public TV) and take any courses you can find that will introduce you to television production. Even if the courses or equipment are not perfect, they will bring you one important step closer to television.

Useful Nontelevision Experience

Useful nontelevision experience that can help prepare you for a job in television includes work in theater, radio, discos, journalism, and politics. Here are some ways you can use these other experiences to prepare you for television work:

- Theater work (school, regional) can help you learn about lighting, audio, directing, producing, writing, staging.
- Radio work can help you learn about producing, news, writing, audio, engineering.
- Newspaper and magazine work can prepare you for TV news writing and producing.
- Disco work can be a good training ground for engineering (audio) and crew work.

- Political work, such as internship with a congressman, can help prepare you for news or public affairs programming.
- Advertising is a good training ground for writers or graphic artists, plus it could get you into TV ad production.

Vendor and Technical Schools

If you can't find an internship or a job where someone will train you to work with specific equipment, take a maintenance or operations course in a technical school or from a manufacturer (vendor) of television equipment. Vendor training is often reasonably priced and high quality, as it is in the manufacturer's best interest to get as many television personnel as possible to know and like their equipment.

Don't limit yourself to learning how to operate equipment—knowing maintenance is invaluable because it will help you understand the equipment, and in smaller stations and production houses you will be expected to maintain the equipment you operate. It's well worth taking a menial job in another field to finance this training. (See Appendix for list of schools.)

Vacation Relief

"Almost everyone I know started out in vacation relief," says one network crew member. Once you've had some kind of experience whether in school, as an intern, volunteer, or for pay, you may be able to find "vacation relief" opportunities. Vacation relief jobs are temporary full-time positions in which you substitute for crew members who are on vacation.

Vacation relief schedules vary from station to station, so you have to call and find out when they are and when they begin accepting applications. While performing vacation relief, you can expect a certain amount of training, but it depends on the size of the station and the nature of the operation.

YOUR RESUME, REEL, AND COVER LETTER

Your resume is your calling card and, in television production, the rules are no different from those for any other kind of job hunting:

- Keep your resume clear, concise, and accurate.
- Write your resume with your audience in mind, include experience that will be useful to them, if necessary prepare two or three resumes for different markets such as news, and corporate/business.
- Fancy typesetting is not essential, though high-quality type-writer (film-ribbon) helps your presentation enormously.
- Make sure there are no spelling or grammatical errors. Check and recheck your resume.
- Duplicate your resume on a photo-quality copying machine.
- Get advice from friends, teachers, and professionals. Ask them to read your resume, listen to their comments, and incorporate those changes you agree with.

Your Reel

Producers, directors, graphic artists, writers, videotape editors, audio and video engineers, camera operators, lighting directors, and other crew members can all benefit from having a reel—a videotape cassette with bits of shows you have worked on. Think of your reel as a video resume. It is your opportunity to show prospective employers what you have done.

Whenever you work on a show, be sure to get a videotaped copy of the program, preferably on a high quality ¾-inch cassette from which you can later edit your resume reel. It is easy to get lazy about making copies, but the chore only gets worse if you wait until you are ready to go job hunting. Of course, as you gain experience, you don't have to save *everything;* you can be selective about what you choose to keep.

There are some basic rules of etiquette about reels that we recommend you observe:

1. Never send an unsolicited reel. Producers and employers don't have room in their offices for more videocassettes. By all means, ask them for permission to send them your reel, but remember that it is an imposition to send them your reel unless they have requested it.
2. Keep your reel short—10 minutes is enough. Remember, television professionals have little free time.

3. If you can, prepare two reels, one with a complete program you worked on and one with a pastiche of programs (your resume reel).

4. Edit your reel professionally. If you can't edit it yourself, ask a friend to edit it for you. Your reel should look professional, but it need not be filled with fancy and costly special effects, unless, of course, you are a graphic artist.

5. Package your reel tastefully. Use a fresh and attractive plastic box to house your reel. Identify it with an attractive label. The label and box are to a reel what a cover is to a book.

6. Bring your reel to your interviews and offer to show it to your interviewer. Do not force it on the interviewer! If the interviewer does ask to see it, be sure to describe precisely your role in the production.

What will your interviewer be looking for in your reel? If you are applying for a producing or associate producing job, your interviewer will be looking for the quality of the script, the way the story is told, the editing, the performance of the talent, and the overall video look and audio sound.

If you are applying for a directing post, the emphasis will be on the use of the camera, the selection and order of shots, the lighting, the performances, and the audio.

As a technical crew member, the interviewer will be looking for evidence of technical quality, depending on your role in the production.

In almost all cases, the interviewer will be interested in the story behind the production. How many cameras did you have? If it was a remote shoot, what were the circumstances and facilities available? How did you work around certain problems? How was the crew? Did you know the other crew and staff members well?

Your Cover Letter

A cover letter is more than just a piece of paper to cover your resume: Your cover letter is an opportunity. Your resume cannot include everything about you. If it did, you'd have difficulty making it concise. The cover letter can add some additional information about you and your background. Another area where the cover letter plays a role is in tailoring your application to the specific program. Making one-of-a-kind resumes for each job you apply for is not practical, but a well planned cover letter can focus the resume.

Your cover letter is a good opportunity to mention specific experience or knowledge that may be useful to your prospective employer. For example, if you are applying to a science program and you have studied science, or participated in science projects or clubs, you can mention it in your letter. Mention your experience with equipment that you know is used frequently where you are applying.

If you are applying for a creative post, you can use the cover letter to say something about the program you are applying for. If you like the show, explain why you like it. If you have an idea for a program, mention it. Or, if you have a suggestion for improving the show, offer it. However, only say something if you mean it and you think it will mean something to your reader.

Here are some general rules about cover letters:

• Type it neatly, using a good typewriter and ribbon.
• Make sure there are no spelling and typing errors.
• Keep it short—no more than one page.
• Write clearly.
• State clearly the kind of job for which you are applying.
• State clearly where, when and how to reach you.
• Spell the addressee's name and title correctly.

THE INTERVIEW

When you prepare for an interview, bear in mind that, more than anything, an interviewer wants to know who you are as a person and what you can learn. Your technical qualifications and production experience are already presented in your resume.

For any type of TV production job, the interviewer will want to know how hard you work, if you can handle long hours, if you will work well in a team, and if you can work well independently. Answer questions with anecdotes and examples that demonstrate your strengths. This applies both to the experienced applicant and the younger applicant fresh out of school (or still there). Even if you don't have much work experience, you can show teamwork through sports or clubs or volunteer work. You can demonstrate leadership, commitment and other qualities through school and summer experiences.

Be prepared for questions about the show you are applying to. "If you are applying for a job at *The Today Show,* watch the show for a month," suggests a Los Angeles network television writer/producer. "Get ideas for segments. Offer ways you could add to the program. For instance, if you have a BA in American literature, you could suggest they do a series on great American authors."

Expect questions about the program's topic—whether you are an artist, a camera operator, or a producer. If you are applying to a news program, you may be asked questions as simple as "Who is the prime minister of England?" The purpose is to hear the way you respond and to double check that you are well-informed.

Of course, there will be technical questions, too, especially if you are an engineer, a videotape editor, or a technical crew member. An audio or video candidate might be asked about the kinds of equipment used, or how to solve a specific equipment failure problem. A lighting person might be asked about types of lighting and how to light in certain situations. But even a producer (or someone hoping to become one) might be asked how he or she would solve a hypothetical production crisis.

Bear in mind that the interviewer is looking for the personal qualities you have that would be helpful for the specific job opening as well as for the nature of the program. Whether you are a technician or a producer, if you apply for work at a news program the interviewer will want to know whether you love news, whether you have a news sense, whether you have the drive and energy to work in a high pressure news environment and hunt down stories. If you are on the creative side of production, the interviewer will also want to know how much you care and know about the program's subject.

Here are some basic tips on how to handle an interview:

- Dress appropriately. If you are applying for a corporate job, try to look corporate—men should wear a tie, women should wear conservative clothing (not pants). If you are applying at a production house, being unconventional may be more appropriate; do some research about the place where you are applying—find out about their style of dress and other things as well.

- Appear relaxed and calm during the interview to convey your ability to handle pressure. Tell an anecdote that shows how coolly you can perform.

- Watch the programs you apply to so that you can intelligently discuss the show, from whatever point of view is appropriate—producing, writing, camera, lighting, audio.

- Show that you are a team player. Give examples whether it's in sports or in a previous job.

- Show that you have initiative. Give examples of projects you launched and followed through to completion.

- If you are introduced to other members of the team, treat each introduction or meeting as being as important as the interview with the person at the top. The interviewer will want to see how well you fit in with the group.

- Interview the interviewer a little, too. Remember that fit is a two-way street; not only do you have to be right for the job, the job has to be right for you. Ask your interviewer about the program, the work atmosphere, even ask if your interviewer likes working for the show. You'll learn something, and the interviewer will probably appreciate your interest and concern for more than just getting a job.

- Show enthusiasm. It's important to let your interviewer know you are interested in the job. However, there's a fine line between letting the interviewer know how much you want the job and coming across like an obsequious puppy dog. Notes a West Coast producer: "Act like you don't want the job, but want it enough internally so that you put your best foot forward. If your tongue is hanging out, people won't take you seriously."

ENTRY LEVEL JOBS THROUGHOUT TV PRODUCTION

Job Opening: Production Assistant—News.

Job Description: Coordinate and communicate information regarding the production of a news program to all involved staff. Responsible for assembling and accuracy of daily program rundowns and logs. Communicate and check for accuracy, all changes in rundown, captions, length of stories, number of graphics and stories. Before program airing, create list of captions, review announcer's script for cues, assure all technical information is received from principal news bureaus.

Requirements: Strong organizational and communication skills. Familiarity with studio control room production. Accuracy. Ability to work under deadline pressure. Knowledge of computers, typing. Journalism as well as college background desirable. Flexible hours.

> *—Based on an actual network news program job posting.*

Regardless of what career you may want to pursue in television production, the beginning is usually the same. What follows are descriptions of the most common entry-level positions, production assistant or intern, and a less common but useful network foot-in-the-door position—a page. There is also a reminder that there are lots of low-level jobs that can help you get started.

Production Assistant/Intern

Whichever title you give it, it's the same job; the only difference is that a production assistant (PA) gets paid—at a very low level—while the intern gets college credit, but not cash.

As a production assistant, you may perform any task from tearing copy off the wire machines, delivering memos, copy, getting coffee and food, substituting for a secretary, doing research. In other words, you will do whatever is necessary.

A production assistant's job is an excellent opportunity for learning, if you keep your eyes open. Learn by watching. Learn, when you can, by doing. Offer as much of your free time as possible—it is during the late or weekend hours that you may be able to prove yourself particularly useful.

At a network or large station, your job might be limited to delivering messages, food, and other nonequipment-oriented tasks, because touching equipment may be strictly the domain of union members in particular job categories.

The greatest opportunity to get hands-on experience is as a production assistant or intern in a small local or cable station or corporate television crew. You may be able to learn how to operate videotape recorders, read audio and video signals, operate a camera, set up lights, handle props, etc. In some cable news operations, including Cable News Network, production assistants (and even interns) are given so much responsibility that they may actually be field producers.

As a production assistant or intern you may find yourself working both in the studio and out in the field on a remote shoot, wrapping cable, assisting with the lighting, viewing raw footage, and noting particularly good sections the editor or producer may want to use when editing the program, and assisting the editor.

Where to Apply

Check with your school career advisory department to see if there is an established internship program for television production. If there isn't, contact all the stations, production houses, and corporate television departments within reasonable commuting distance, to determine if they have an internship program and, if so, who heads it. If not, write to the producer of individual television programs (check the credits at the end of the show to find the name of the producer and the studio name), or the head of the corporate television department (often a vice president).

Follow the newspapers and industry journals for information about new programs—start-up programs are particularly good places to find a production assistant or intern spot and get a lot of responsibility in the job.

For private television opportunities, contact your local chapter of the International Television Association (ITVA). The ITVA can tell you about private television internships and entry-level job possibilities in nonbroadcast television such as corporate television departments, government agencies and others. See the list of associations in the appendix of this book for the address and phone number of the ITVA's international headquarters.

Starting as a Page

Ted Koppel, anchor of ABC's *Nightline,* was one. David Hartman, co-anchor of ABC's *Good Morning America,* was one. The actor Ken Howard (*Dynasty* and *The Colbys*), and meteorologist Willard Scott (NBC's *Today Show*) were also.

Pages are the entry-level, salaried temporary positions available at the three major networks (ABC, CBS, NBC) as well as at some of the network owned and operated stations (in New York, Los Angeles, Chicago, etc.) and select major market independent stations. Generally, you should be a college graduate to qualify. As a page you will have the opportunity to work in a variety of departments in a television network.

What kind of work will you actually do? At NBC network in New York, you might give one of the famous NBC studio tours, monitor the reception line for the public who is coming to be the audience for a show such as *Saturday Night Live* or *The David Letterman Show.* As a page, you might find your duties ranging from filling in for the receptionist for the news room or the vacationing secretary in documentaries, to delivering copy and teleprompter script.

The idea behind a page job is that, within the nine or more months of your employment, you will gain exposure to a variety of departments and will make enough contacts to help you land a job at the network. Sometimes the job offer comes while you are still a page; sometimes a few months later. The system definitely works, as many major executives and network professionals who began as pages can attest.

Do your job, no matter how menial, as well as you can. Make contacts, let people know you are interested in their department (if you are), study the job posting bulletin boards and apply for anything appropriate, ask a lot of questions, make friends with secretaries, who often have the inside scoop on openings.

Watch for any promotions in departments that interest you because promotions have a trickle-down effect in networks: Since they have a policy of hiring from within, one promotion leads to another until a production assistant or desk assistant spot ends up vacant.

Where to Apply

Contact the three major networks (ABC, CBS, NBC) in New York and Los Angeles and their owned and operated stations where they produce their own programming; also contact other major market stations such as those in the new Fox Television network. Ask for the name of the manager of the pages. Write to the manager and send your resume with a cover letter.

Librarian/Researcher/Runner/Secretary/Audience Relations/Other

There is a host of foot-in-the-door jobs available in television. This is especially true in the networks and other large television production places. The key, however, once you get one is not to get stuck there.

Where to Apply

Contact the personnel or human resources department at the major broadcast and cable networks and apply for anything. In your cover letter you should highlight any skills, such as secretarial, telephone work or research, that they may find useful.

Contact individual departments where your skills may be useful, such as the library department, and contact directly the executive producer of the shows where you particularly want to work—a news show, a talk show, etc.

3

The Production Crew

- **Technical Director**
- **Floor/Stage Manager**
- **Camera Operator**
- **Lighting Director**
- **Set/Scenic Designer**
- **Audio Engineer**
- **Video Engineer**

These people are the flesh and bones of television producing. The most brilliant producer, erudite director, and inspired writer are nothing without them—indeed, you can't produce a television show without them.

Depending on the size and scope of a production, the production crew can range from a small ad hoc group of people wielding a camera with some lights to a large crowd of highly specialized individuals who operate like an army.

This chapter will describe the career paths in television production and how you can begin a career in this area of the medium. To begin, let's briefly describe what the crew is and does.

The Crew versus the Staff

The people behind the screen of a TV program fall into two groups (although the line is often blurred in a small operation): production *staff* members and production *crew* members. The *staff* members are those considered to be creative—

the producer, director, writer, production assistants, and others. Since the *crew* members work primarily with the production equipment, they are considered to be technicians—although that term does not accurately reflect the creativity and ingenuity they bring to their work. The crew members include: the technical director, audio engineer, video engineer, camera operator, floor/stage manager, set designer, lighting director, and a variety of technicians.

The crew and the staff are often referred to as "below the line" and "above the line," respectively. These terms are budgetary terms; "below the line" are those production personnel who physically produce the program and are therefore part of a fixed cost just as equipment or studio rentals are. "Above the line" refers to the creative personnel. These distinctions are not as black and white as they may sound. Both crew and staff members must be creative, and there is considerable overlap between the two groups. In fact, at some stations camera operators are considered technicians while at others they are seen as part of the production staff. At different stations, a position may be considered part of engineering or part of production.

ESSENTIALS FOR THE JOB

Whether production crew people are "tekkies" involved in the technological aspect of their jobs or people more involved in the aesthetics of their function, they share several important qualifications. Production crew members must know their equipment both on a technological and functional level—how it works and what it can do. Ideally they possess a thorough understanding of the function of the entire crew and production process.

They should be detail-oriented. When even one element is off, the whole production is affected and time can be lost. And in television production, time really is money.

Crew members must be good communicators and team players. You can have a lighting designer with the best lighting, a set designer who has created a gorgeous set and a costume designer whose work is breathtaking. But if they haven't coordinated their act, you can have disaster: the beautiful set is made of a material that causes reflections and distorts the lighting; the flashy patterns and brilliant colors of the costumes send ripples and distortion effects across the video screen; and the lighting designer's artillery of lights contains everything you need for lighting anything but a glossy reflecting set.

Crew members need aesthetic creativity, and they need ingenuity. They should have a knack for solving problems quickly and imaginatively. Equipment fails, surprise situations arise, and the crew members—like an army—have to be ready for anything and everything.

Finally, crew members need physical stamina that goes beyond what it takes to set up and move heavy production equipment. They should be able to survive—and even thrive—on a schedule that can demand work at all hours including marathonlike stints round the clock or one of shift changes—two weeks of working nights on one production can be followed by two weeks of working days or early mornings for another. The effect of sudden changes of shift is like the worst kind of jet lag, and its effect on your personal life can be equally devastating.

The crew needs cast-iron stomachs, too. They're going to be subsisting on a lot of fast-food meals at weird hours. As one corporate television producer said: "To be in this business you have to be able to eat a cold take-out hamburger and a warm Coke—and enjoy it."

There is one aspect of the television industry that affects crew members in every job at just about every level. Keep it in mind when you are weighing where to apply for a position because it will help you determine what to expect from the job you are seeking:

There are advantages and disadvantages to working either at a network, large production company, or other upscale operation, or at a local, cable or other relatively small operation such as a corporate video department.

In the big time, you have a chance to see a smorgasbord of the latest state-of-the-art equipment, while at the smaller, "poorer" organization, the equipment will be less sophisticated, not as new, and sometimes even minimal.

But at the network studio, you may be constrained to stay rigidly within your job description because of union rules and just plain bigness. You may not even be able to touch the fancy equipment—literally—much less learn to operate it outside of your job. While at the smaller place, you'll have the opportunity to do a variety of jobs and to use any equipment you are willing to learn. You will also have to call on your ingenuity and imagination to come up with good answers to problems where the conventional solutions are too expensive.

THE CREW AT WORK: IN THE STUDIO AND OUT ON LOCATION

A typical studio production facility consists of two basic production areas: the control room and the studio floor. The control room is the room where the producer, director, associate director, technical director, audio engineer, video engineer, and production assistant work. The studio floor is the place where the production actually takes place.

Inside the control room are video monitors; a production console that includes the technical director's (TD) switcher; a separate glassed-in booth for the audio engineer and audio control console; a separate section for the video engineers and their camera control units (sometimes the video control area is separate from the main control room).

While sometimes the studio floor is in direct view of the control room window, this is not always the case. The floor is an open area in which the set, television cameras, microphones, lighting, and other equipment are set up. It is where the performers, floor/stage manager, producers, production assistants, camera operators, lighting crew, and other technicians work.

Location productions fall into three basic categories: electronic news gathering (ENG), electronic field production (EFP), and multiple-camera remote production. These differ in complexity and in the scope for pre-planning that they offer. ENG is news and is generally spontaneous. EFP is a fancy expression that covers shoots outside the studio involving one camera, such as an interview with a corporate executive in his or her office, or an interview with a celebrity at home. A multiple-camera remote production could be for a magazine show or documentary where the action requires coverage by more than one camera. Using more than one camera enables a producer to liven up a filming of a conference as, for example, by capturing speakers on one camera and audience on another and cutting between them.

Whether the on-location (also called "remote") production is simple or complex, it generally involves portable cameras and equipment, and a truck or van (called a mobile truck) to carry the equipment for the taping. A mobile truck can be a simple van that the crew loads up with equipment or a complex customized vehicle.

THE CREW MEMBERS AND THEIR ROLES

While the section of this chapter on career paths goes into detail about production crew jobs, here are brief descriptions of the job functions of the principal members of a crew. The specific jobs do not always exist as separate positions. In smaller productions many crew members double and triple in their functions, with the camera operator doubling as the lighting director and the video engineer also handling audio.

The Technical Director

The technical director (TD) is responsible for the technical aspects of a production and for the crew and their technical performance. The technical director works directly for the director—in fact, they usually sit side-by-side in the control room during production. The TD operates the video switcher—an electronic device used to select the image, make composite images and/or special visual effects requested by the director. In some productions where the only function of the TD is operating the switcher, then the job title is simply "the switcher." Because timing and accuracy of execution are critical, the job of technical directing can be a high-pressure one—especially in live broadcasts.

Floor/Stage Manager

Since the director of a production works from the control room and sees the studio floor and its personnel only through a monitor, there must be someone acting as the eyes, ears, and voice of the director. That someone is the floor/stage manager, who becomes the focal point of any production. During production, this crew member gives hand signals to indicate timing (five seconds remaining, hurry up), audio cues (speak louder, softer) to the on-stage talent (whether actors, hosts or guests) and to various other members of the production and crew. Ultimately, the stage/floor manager is responsible for the placement of all personnel and props—a considerable task in any size production.

Camera Operator

The camera operator is responsible for operating the cameras whether in the studio or on location (remote shoot). Often, the camera person works with the video engineer to set and align the studio cameras as well. In smaller operations, the operator often runs more than one camera simultaneously. He or she may use a camera that is mounted on a stationary tripod, one that is mounted on a dolly to allow movement while shooting, or a portable camera. Framing or composition of the video image and camera movement are the principal responsibilities of the camera operator during a shoot.

Lighting Director

The lighting director is responsible for lighting a television production, whether it is shot indoors or out. Lighting design can range from simple to sophisticated, ad hoc to computerized high tech. The lighting of a TV show has three basic purposes—functional, aesthetic, and dramatic. Lighting should illuminate the subject adequately—that's functional. It can do a lot to make the camera image attractive—an aesthetic contribution. And, lighting, like music, can be used to create dramatic effects and add to the emotional atmosphere of a television drama or comedy.

Set/Scenic Designer

The set/scenic designer, sometimes called the art director, creates the design for the sets for television productions. For a news show, this may involve only a one-shot job; the news set is used for every show and requires nothing more than maintenance on a regular basis. For entertainment, obviously, set design is more elaborate and is comparable to work in theater and theatrical film. The set/scenic designer supervises the stagehands and crew members who construct or assemble the set in the studio.

Audio Engineer

The audio engineer, sometimes called the audio control engineer, is in charge of the production's sound both in studio production and on location. The audio engineer's responsibilities include preparing the audio equipment and facilities—the audio console, microphones, tape recorders, audio turntable, and also the communications systems for the production personnel. The audio engineer supervises the audio crew if he or she isn't all of it, and the production is large enough to warrant an audio crew. During studio production, the audio engineer sits in the control room at an audio console mixing the sound from all sources—from microphones to remote feeds—to create the final mixed sound of the program.

Video Engineer

The video engineer, sometimes called video control engineer, is responsible for the quality of the picture itself. In preparation for studio production, the video engineer sets up and aligns the cameras (sometimes this is done together with the camera operator) for best picture quality. Technically, this is known as "registering the camera." During studio production, the video engineer sits in the control room near large screen monitors and a console with controls to adjust the contrast, brightness, and color balance of each camera.

A DAY WITH THE TV CREW

The daily work of a crew member varies depending on the type of television program and where it is produced. Production at a small station in a tiny market is a totally different experience from production at a network. News is different from entertainment production. Studio news is different from news on location.

Entertainment production in a studio is also different from its counterpart on location. There are also different challenges when shooting or lighting a game show, a situation comedy, or a soap opera. And there are different challenges in producing a show that is being taped for later airing from one that airs live. In other words, there are as many different types of production situations as there are television programs.

It is this richness of production types that makes television so interesting and challenging. Nonetheless, there are enough common threads to be able to give you several more or less "typical" days of crew members at work.

A Day With . . .

An Audio Engineer on *The David Letterman Show*

> The David Letterman Show, *broadcast at night on the NBC network, is produced at NBC's Rockefeller Center, New York City studios. The show is pre-recorded at 5:30 in the afternoons for airing at a later time. The audio person has four main concerns during rehearsal and taping: sound from the boom microphones; music (the jazz band's amplifier); David Letterman's microphone; the area beside the band, where most acts perform during the show.*

9:30 AM

The audio engineer begins work at the studio, doing a technical checkup of equipment: the audio console, the microphones, the lines for transmissions, the tape machines, the sound from the show's live musical band. This check can take about two hours.

11:30 AM

Production meeting, attended by the director, producer, writers, floor/stage manager, audio engineer, video engineer, camera operators, and others. They go over the script, the guest list, the acts, the production elements necessary, including requests for particular types of background music or sound effects. Most of these effects and bits of music have been ordered in advance, and it's merely a question of getting the elements in order or editing a piece of music to length.

12:30 PM

Lunch break.

1:30 PM

The audio crew—sound effects person, an audio tape person, two audio assistants—assembles necessary elements.

2:30 PM

Two-hour rehearsal. The entire show is run through—all skits, all monologues, all music. During the rehearsal, as during the taping of the show, the audio person is in contact with the technical director (TD) through the private line headset. The TD gives instructions about how many seconds until the next skit and audio effect, lets the crew know if there are any changes in the show sequence, etc.

4:30 PM

Break.

5:30 PM

Recording of the show. (Details of how a show is recorded are given in the descriptions of various crew jobs later in this chapter.)

Three Days With . . .

The Crew for *Kate and Allie*

This CBS situation comedy is produced in New York City at the Ed Sullivan Theater by Reeves Teletape. The technical director is also the chief engineer for Reeves who puts on the TD hat three days a week for production of this show. As chief engineer the rest of the week, he is in charge of all engineers and the purchasing of equipment. As TD, he is in charge of the crew and operates the switcher.

Day One

7 AM

TD arrives, makes sure the control room equipment is on and functioning, and that the air conditioning is operating.

9 AM

The rest of the crew—audio engineer, video engineer, lighting director, camera operators, stage manager—arrives. The TD counts noses to see if everyone is there. The crew spends the first hour setting up equipment and organizing props.

10 AM

Rehearsal with performers to establish blocking (the actors' movement on the set) for camera angles and lighting and to check audio and video. (The actors have been rehearsing for the two previous days without cameras and equipment.) The crew has copies of the script that indicates where each camera, light, and audio effect should be at what line of dialogue. The TD operates the switcher according to the director's requests and also points out problems observed on the monitor. The video engineer checks the quality of the video and looks for boom shadows from the microphones. The audio engineer checks the quality of the audio and monitors the execution of any special effects (doors slamming, car motors revving, etc.). The stage manager supervises the props and signals the performers according to the director's requests over the private line (PL), though the director may talk directly to the performers over a public address system.

1 PM

Lunch break.

2 PM

Blocking rehearsal resumes.

4:30 PM

Another rehearsal with cameras, attended by CBS executives and compliance lawyers who critique the show to make sure there are no legal problems.

6 PM

Rehearsal over. The crew puts away equipment.

Day Two

The second day of crew rehearsal is a repeat of the first.

Day Three

The third day of crew rehearsal is also the shooting day for the show.

7 AM

TD arrives and checks control room equipment and air conditioning.

9 AM

Crew sets up equipment.

10 AM

Blocking rehearsal with cameras and equipment.

2 PM

Lunch.

3 PM

Crew prepares equipment and props for show.

3:30 PM

Live studio audience arrives. A stand-up comedian warms up the audience by telling jokes.

4 PM

First taping of show. The taping takes approximately an hour-and-a-half because the scenes are performed in proper sequence (so that the audience understands the story) necessitating moving the performers and crew to different sets. Scenes are sometimes shot two or three times for technical and performance reasons.

5:30 PM

Second audience arrives for second taping of the show. Comedian warms up the audience.

6 PM

Second taping and performance of the show. The second taping is generally the one used in the broadcast of the program. However, parts of the first taping may be spliced in if those scenes are better.

7:30 PM

Second taping over. Crew puts away equipment.

A Day With . . .

A Corporate Television Crew

> In most corporate video departments, crew members double up on their roles. There is usually no need for a floor manager, set designer, or lighting designer, and it generally isn't affordable to have them. Generally, lights will be used, but their use is straightforward and can be handled by a general crew member.

6 AM

Camera operator, who doubles as van driver, picks up the engineer who handles both audio and video, and they go to the studio. They meet the show producer, the production assistant, and the editor who on production days acts as lighting assistant and make-up person. The crew loads the van with the camera, lights and other equipment.

They drive to company headquarters for "facility set up" (FAX) in order to shoot an interview with a company executive for a monthly company news program.

7 AM

The crew arrives at the executive office and sets up lights and camera. They adjust shades and move plants behind the desk to add color. A production assistant sits in the executive's chair while the camera operator focuses and takes light readings.

8 AM

The executive to be interviewed arrives and is made-up by the editor/makeup/lighting person. The audio person clips a little lavalier microphone to the executive's lapel.

8:30 AM

Producer interviews the executive. Several questions are asked twice because of audio problems, the executive stumbles over words, or the camera operator isn't pleased with camera movements or framing. During the taping, the audio/video person is watching a wave-form monitor to check the signals coming out of the camera, listening to the audio with audio headsets, and checking a monitor to make sure the video quality is good. During taping, the production assistant codes the questions and answers with elapsed time and notes specific sections that the producer indicates are a "buy"— good bits of interview that will likely be used in the final production.

10 AM

Interview completed, the crew takes candid shots of the executive talking on the phone, talking to other people and doing paperwork. These shots can be used for library footage (video that may not be necessary for the program being produced that day but kept on file for later re-use) and for "cutaways," or footage with voice-over to cover up editing cuts in the final video. The engineer tapes office sound in case it is needed later in the edit. This can be useful if the executive wants to change a sentence and is retaped on another day; the extra office sound can be mixed with the re-taping and made to "match" the original taping.

The crew also shoots footage of the office, the building, people working, and signs identifying the location. Since the crew is already there, it is important to make the most of the opportunity and contribute to the library footage for future video use.

12 Noon

Crew breaks for lunch, packs up the equipment, and goes to the next shoot.

1 PM

The van goes out to the street and to another company-owned building. The crew's assignment is to shoot exteriors of the building for the video department's video library. The production assistant logs tape, marking on the tape where certain images are being recorded.

2:30 PM

Crew goes into the building to tape the host of the company's monthly news program. A vendor specializing in set construction and maintenance delivers and sets up the regular set for the show. This set is a desk/podium with a backdrop showing the program's logo.

All crew members are given marked copies of the anchor person's script. The makeup person applies makeup to the anchor while the crew sets up lights and equipment.

During shooting, the producer directs the anchor's "performance," requesting additional takes as necessary. The makeup person monitors the state of the anchor's makeup and touches up the anchor's face if sweat and hot lights are causing a shine.

There are moments during the anchor's talk when scenes will appear in a Quantel box—a video screen that viewers will see above the anchor's shoulder. The camera operator must be sure to get both the anchor and the video box in the picture at these points, which are marked on the script. The picture in the Quantel box will be added after the show is taped. Since the camera operator can't operate camera and read the script at the same time, the video person cues the camera movements by tugging at the operator's pants leg.

A production assistant will probably be checking audio and logging tape. Another production assistant may be running a teleprompter in case the anchor needs it.

5 PM

The crew packs up and returns to the studio. Equipment is removed from the van and locked up. Tapes are filed.

CAREER PATHS FOR TV PRODUCTION CREW MEMBERS

Unless there is one specific aspect of television production that really appeals to you, the ideal is to learn all aspects of production from the bottom up. Learning all the technical elements of television production will help you enormously for a career in whatever specialty you choose.

Once you have learned the ropes of television production, you are not limited to a career as a specialist in one of the functions highlighted in this chapter; you will also be qualified to pursue—and with luck and perseverance get—producing and directing jobs. In fact, your technical knowledge and prowess can be an enormous advantage over those who have taken the "creative" route as writers and placed their emphasis on the story being produced rather than how it is done.

Descriptions of the various jobs along the television production path follow. The jobs are not necessarily treated in the order in which you might get them or must get them. Television production jobs vary from place to place; how you move to better positions is an individual matter, often more the result of good luck and timing than the existence of any rigid career ladder.

The job descriptions include information about the jobs themselves, requirements, the differences in network, local, cable, and corporate television, and where to apply. But in many television production situations jobs may not be as differentiated as they are in this list. Many production crew jobs will be rolled into one and given vague titles such as "engineer" or "studio field engineer," that are just fancy names for "Jack (or Jill) of all television trades."

How to Apply

The procedure for applying for any crew position is virtually the same. What exceptions there are will be mentioned after the individual job descriptions. In every case, the first step is to telephone the place where you're interested in working and get the name and title of the person who hires for the specific job you want. Depending on the job you are looking for and the setup of the particular studio or station, you'll be told to get in touch with someone with a title such as the chief engineer, the studio operations manager, the production manager, or the manpower/scheduling manager.

At corporations with private television departments, contact either the director or corporate vice president in charge of video, audio/visual or communications. If the department is very large it may have someone at the head of technical production. Contact your local chapter of the International Television Association (ITVA) for the names of managers or directors of corporate television or video departments near you. However, crew for many private/corporate television productions are hired on a freelance basis.

Production Assistant, Intern and Other Entry-Level Jobs

See Chapter 2, "How to Begin Your TV Production Career," for information about these jobs.

Production Associate

Often confused with production assistant, the job of production associate (also termed PA) is quite different. Not an entry-level position, the job is actually that of assistant in the control room, and as such is sometimes differentiated from PA by the terms *master control PA* or *program associate*.

As an assistant to the associate director (AD), you fetch and carry for the AD and the director, but you also act as assistant in a more exalted sense. As a master control PA, you sit in the control room at the side of the associate director (AD) and follow your boss's actions regarding timing segments and keeping notes, taking notes on camera shots and sequences that the director has specified. Ideally, should the AD walk out of the room, you should be able to perform the AD's job. In fact, as master control PA, you are next in line for training as an AD, and may (if you are experienced enough) act as substitute AD when the AD is away from the job.

Where to Apply

The position of production associate is generally one you are promoted into from the position of production assistant. For information about where to apply see Chapter 2. Once you are a production assistant, be sure to get to know the director and AD as they will play a key role in a promotion to production associate. You could also apply directly to specific directors; a great cover letter can sometimes get you an interview, but most directors expect you to have previous production experience as a production assistant.

Should politics keep you out of the running for an associate's job (after all there is only one control room for each program), consider getting another PA job for another program at your station, or go to another station (perhaps a smaller one) and start all over. Or go to a much smaller environment where you might start as a crew member or even an AD.

Audio Technician

An assistant to the audio engineer, this position is usually only available in large market television stations and big production houses. As an assistant to the audio engineer, you may specialize in setting up the microphones required for a production, holding the boom microphone before a live audience to pick up audience sounds (applause, laughter, etc.), or supervising the amplifier or sound systems.

Requirements for the job of audio technician include previous experience in radio or television production and/or other audio experience. Experience in a rock-and-roll band handling the recording, the public address system, or the sound system is valuable training for audio technician work.

Where to Apply

This (and other crew jobs) may be handled by the engineering department or the production/studio operation department. As a rule of thumb, expect complicated titles and specialization in the networks. As a result, there might be several departments through which you could apply for an audio position.

Audio Engineer

The audio engineer in television is what the radio engineer was before TV existed. The audio engineer is responsible for the sound of a television production in both studio and remote situations. Sound in a video production can range from the speech of actors and talent to ambient sound such as traffic or the sound of kids laughing in a playground.

The audio engineer has responsibilities both before and during production. In pre-production, the audio engineer scouts out the location or studio to determine the audio requirements of the setting and maps out what audio equipment—from microphones to amplifiers—is necessary, where it can be set up, and how it can be wired without impeding other aspects of the production.

At production time, the audio engineer sets up and operates the audio consoles, microphones, tape recorders, audio turntable, and audio tapes cut and edited for sound effects.

In a studio production, the audio engineer, working at a console in the audio booth, mixes the various audio inputs to balance them and create the final mixed sound of the program.

Television audio also includes the vital communication systems of the production crew. In studio settings, the audio crew is responsible for the functioning and set up of the private line through which the director communicates with the crew outside the control room.

In some field productions—such as live sports coverage and news—audio communications for the crew is vastly more complex than the audio setup for the actual broadcast. In a baseball game, for example, the audio on the air is basically two guys talking and a bat mike. The field setup, though, is more complicated. As many as 50 people in the crew have to talk to each other. So, the audio crew spends a couple of days before the sports event setting up a system allowing the people in the production truck to talk to the people in the booth.

In news production on location, the audio engineer's role includes using microphones to get ambient sound, or random background noise. The audio engineer may also be responsible for carrying the video cassette recorder, operating it, replacing cassettes as necessary, and monitoring the sound/audio levels of the recording.

Where to Apply
See general tips on applying for crew jobs on page 52.

Video Engineer
The video engineer is the person responsible for the actual look of a television picture. The video engineer must work closely with the camera operator and the lighting director because their work is interdependent. (Video engineering is excellent training for camera and lighting work.)

The video engineer's pre-production responsibilities include the set up of the camera and the proper registration of the video and camera levels. "In addition to proper registration," a network engineer explains, "if the cameras are computer controlled, the video operator will have to run the camera through the computer camera sequence. What this means is that the camera's values—white scale and color—are programmed into the computer and the camera has to be adjusted to match its computer-set values. Once this is done, the camera should be ready for the show."

The video engineer's production responsibilities are primarily to monitor the levels of the cameras during a shoot. If more than one camera is used, the video engineer must also "match" the cameras to be sure the video levels are the same in all cameras being used. So, as a director switches from camera to camera, the color, brightness, and darkness levels all look the same and the viewer doesn't see the production as a patchwork quilt.

During a shoot, the video operator's work also includes adjusting the cameras according to the different lighting. This is a function particularly important in shows where lighting changes for dramatic reasons.

"In entertainment programs—particularly soap operas," observes an engineer, "lighting . . . can be an important part of the show itself. The video operator has to adjust or 'paint' the cameras to make sure that the look, such as the color balances, that the director seeks is obtained." In news programs, where the lighting is uniform throughout the show, the video operator does not have to be so concerned with lighting adjustments.

An additional challenge for the video operator working on dramatic programs is that camera movement from light to dark stage areas may necessitate video adjustments. The video engineer must be familiar with the script and planned camera movements and must be ready to compensate for changes in lighting so the taped image is clear and not muddy.

Video engineering opportunities can vary widely, depending on the size and scope of a television production. At its most complex, video engineering work can be extremely challenging, especially during a shoot involving many cameras. Basic studio setups require from three to five cameras that must be matched, and major sports events can involve matching as many as 20 cameras!

In smaller productions—a news program at a small local station, a corporate television department—video engineering as a specialty may not exist. Rather, the video engineer may double as the audio engineer, or in an extremely small setup, the video engineering responsibilities may belong to a general crew member who also handles lighting or some other aspect of production.

Where to Apply

See the general information about where to apply for crew jobs on page 52. The title of video engineer exists in corporate television only in a very large department; the more generic audio/video engineering position exists in smaller settings and is likely to be freelance.

Assistant Camera Operator

The assistant camera operator is not an entry-level position, but provides a good way for a person with camera experience in a non-network environment to get a foot in the door in a large television production. In a studio setting, the assistant camera operator's responsibilities include helping to register the camera (see description of Camera Operator's job for more details), and making sure that cameras can physically move into required positions on the set floor during the shoot. During production, the assistant, following the directions of the camera operator, moves the dolly holding the camera and the operator.

In both studio and nonstudio work such as news gathering, if the camera is carried on the camera operator's shoulders, the assistant will carry cables and clear obstacles from the camera operator's path permitting camera operator to shoot without interruption. In news production outside the studio, the assistant also acts as a traffic cop and keeps the interview or shooting area free of passersby and other distractions.

Where to Apply

See page 52.

Camera Operator

Being a camera operator can range from highly creative work to highly technical work. It all depends on the production situation and the level of responsibility and independence the director permits.

Basically, the camera operator is responsible for the set up and operation of television cameras at a shoot and for the framing or composition of the video image and camera movement. Images have to be framed so the necessary elements are visible and balanced, and camera movement should be smooth and natural. If a camera operator zooms into a close-up of a person talking, the zoom must be smooth and not require a sudden disorienting refocus once the zoom is completed.

The challenge of a camera operator's job varies widely according to the production. One camera operator, who has covered everything from sports to entertainment specials, finds sports easy "because all you have to do is follow a hockey puck or a football." But shooting a situation comedy is harder: "You have to follow that script, and the camera has to be in a certain spot when a character reaches the refrigerator, and you just can't afford to get lost." Other camera operators disagree and say sports are more challenging to shoot.

In terms of creativity, a dramatic show shot in a studio may put the camera operator in a position of following commands rather than initiating creative moves. There will be several cameras in use, and the director usually determines the camera movements in advance of the shooting. If this makes the camera operator's job sound mechanical and unchallenging, consider the fact that the operator also has to have perfect timing and must follow the script precisely. The camera has to be on the actor's face the moment the actor says a specific line. It is demanding work.

In some situations, the camera operator also gets involved with the cinematography. He or she participates in the planning of the camera angles and camera movement at the preproduction stage.

In electronic journalism (EJ), the camera operator has more autonomy and plays a different role. The producer or reporter in charge of the crew indicates what needs to be shot for the story, but the camera operator decides on the camera movements, on the framing, on whether or not to zoom in on the subject's fidgeting hands or sweaty brow, or whether to pan a group of people in a demonstration.

The EJ camera operator may even act in the role of a journalist and assist in discovering the story—pointing out events that the reporter didn't notice and literally running after a story. Many camera operators covering wars and other disasters are known for bravery and determination.

Camera operating jobs vary widely in terms of responsibility, depending on the size of the station or production facility. A camera operator in a small station may have several jobs in addition to running the camera. The camera operator may run two cameras simultaneously for the six o'clock news. (The camera operator just stands between the two cameras, one of which may be used for close-ups only while the other is for wide shots, and adjusts the angles when necessary.) After the news, this operator may go to videotape and run that area and then at 10 PM run master control, and at midnight, sign off the transmitter for the station and, finally, go home.

The main requirement for a position as a camera operator is—previous experience as a camera operator! You can get this experience by learning camera operation as a video engineer or technician or by befriending the camera operator and managing to get training so you can act as substitute camera operator when the operator is on vacation or out sick.

Where to Apply
See page 52.

Lighting Person

This job is available almost exclusively in large markets and production companies where productions are complex. (Often, a production assistant or other general crew member assigned to the lighting director functions as a lighting person without the title.) As a lighting person, you are expected to have experience in lighting (perhaps even as a lighting director) in a smaller operation, though a lucky applicant could get on-the-job training.

The responsibilities of the lighting person include executing the orders of the lighting director, setting up lights according to direction, taking light-meter readings of certain areas of a set or of the performers, maintaining the lighting equipment, reordering equipment and parts, and putting away the equipment after its use.

Where to Apply

Apply for lighting assistant positions at large stations in major markets, the networks, and major production companies. Contact unions such as IATSE for information about job opportunities.

Lighting Director

The lighting director is responsible for lighting a television production, whether it is shot indoors or out. In large markets, at the network level, and major production studios responsible for network programming such as series and dramatic specials, the position of lighting director is a major one involving sophisticated and sometimes computerized systems. In smaller markets, such as cable and local stations and in corporate television departments, there is no formal lighting director, and a general crew member handles lighting.

Before actual production, the lighting director designs the lighting for a studio show by studying a floor plan of the set and the script and determines how to achieve appropriate lighting effects. The lighting director selects the types of lights necessary and decides where to place them on the set and in the studio. For on-location shoots, the lighting director might scout the location in advance or, in the case of news coverage indoors (in an office environment, for example), will simply bring basic lights and hope for the best.

Lighting work during the actual production varies considerably. A dramatic program will require specific types of lighting at specific times in the script—for example, a spot may have to follow a performer moving across the stage, or the dramatic mood may require special lighting effects. In this case, the lighting director would supervise a crew to install and position the lights in accordance with the design. And, during the shoot itself, the lighting director would either operate the lighting control board or cue a lighting control operator in doing it.

As lighting director, or a member of a lighting crew, your responsibilities also include maintaining the department's lights, purchasing equipment, and performing routine maintenance.

Lighting is an element of production that all crew members should know how to handle—especially camera operators since their work is directly dependent upon the quality of lighting. In fact, as a career path, camera work and lighting work can interconnect; camera operators can move into lighting as a specialty, and lighting directors can move into cinematography.

Where to Apply

A good source of information about job opportunities is unions that represent lighting directors—IATSE, for example. Generally, lighting director jobs are available only in large operations. To obtain work as a freelance lighting director for corporate television, you might present yourself as a general crew member with lighting expertise or as a lighting expert to be hired for lighting assignments only.

Second Stage Manager

Second stage managers (or assistant stage managers) are generally found in large-scale prime-time productions. For example, at *The Cosby Show* in New York there is one full-time second stage manager who hires one or two additional second stage managers only when there are large groups of extras on the show who need managing. On the other hand, a small news production, with one plain set, little stage movements, and only a few performers or talent to cue, probably does not need a second stage manager.

A second stage manager is the stage manager's assistant in a very real sense. He or she does what the regular stage manager does, acting as the director on the stage floor and shares many of the stage managing responsibilities with the stage manager. The difference between the two jobs is that the stage manager supervises the second stage manager.

If the stage or sets are large enough, the second stage manager may share cueing responsibilities with the stage manager.

For example, the second stage manager cues the performers who make their entrances at the part of the stage farthest from the audience, while the stage manager handles all the downstage cues. Or the second stage manager may have the job of making sure all the performers are costumed and made-up on time.

A second stage manager in prime-time production may also have responsibility for casting extras and stand-ins. As the director on the floor, the second stage manager may also transmit instructions to the actors from the director in the control booth. How much the second (or first) stage manager elaborates on these directions depends on the style and attitude of the show's director.

To get a second stage managing position, you should have significant crew or production experience. It's best to start out by getting a promotion from within—usually from production assistant. There are always stories of lucky people who get trained on the job, and while you shouldn't count on luck, you should also not rule it out.

Where to Apply

Apply for the position of second stage manager directly to the stage manager or to the director of a specific program. The stage manager generally is the person who hires. Contact the Directors Guild of America which often has information about freelance and full-time job opportunities.

Stage/Floor Manager

The position of stage/floor manager is not an entry-level one. Its prerequisites include experience as a crew member in several functions and managerial experience as well. For example, having been a lighting director supervising a lighting crew, or a video engineer directing a crew of technicians, would help qualify you. In general, it is a position that you can get promoted into from being a crew member, perhaps after acting as a vacation relief stage/floor manager.

A stage or floor manager (the terms are used interchangeably) manages all activity on the production stage/floor. "The director on the floor," a network stage manager calls the job, as opposed to a director in the control booth, who often is out of visual contact with the crew and staff during production. The stage/floor manager acts as the director's eyes, ears, and voice. Through the private line headset and mouth microphone, they communicate with each other throughout the program's rehearsals and live airing or taping.

"As stage manager, I'm the production liaison between the director and talent and everything else on the floor—the camera operators, stage hands, anyone that's out there," the network stage manager says. "As stage manager, you are in charge of everyone and everything—props, graphics, teleprompter, crew, talent, guests, where and when they should go. You even have to accommodate everyone in terms of dressing rooms."

The stage manager may be responsible for details ranging from seeing that the talent gets a glass of water, to telling the talent where to stand and when to face which camera and from what angle.

Pre-production responsibilities include supervising the staging, the set up of scenery and all production-related equipment. The floor/stage manager also works with the set/scenic designer during construction, painting and assembly of the set and makes certain that the props have been ordered and have arrived.

The floor/stage manager is the only crew member who can communicate with the talent on stage. Union regulations in larger productions dictate this rule for very practical (in addition to arcane job jurisdiction) reasons: During the production, one centralized source of information for the talent on stage significantly reduces chaos.

During taping and rehearsals, the floor/stage manager is the person who cues the talent and guests and gives them other instructions that the producer and director may want to convey. For example, using hand signals, cue boards (large cards with instructions) or timing cues such as "three minutes to go," the stage manager will speed a segment up, or slow it down.

Similarly, if during a talk show a guest has made a comment that the producer thinks should be followed up by the host, the producer will hand the floor/stage manager a large hand-printed cue board that reads "Don't let him get away with that question," and the manager will flash that card for the host to read.

Floor/stage manager work exists in almost all television productions except for very small cable stations or corporate television departments. In smaller settings, the stage/floor manager is a general crew member who is assigned various aspects of production responsibility, and the director of the production may be the one to give hand and timing signals.

Where to Apply

Apply to a show's director or producer. Be sure to check with the Directors Guild of America and AFTRA for information about full-time, part-time, and freelance job opportunities.

Scenic Artist

The prerequisite for becoming a scenic designer is being a scenic artist—the person who actually executes the designer's instructions. Scenic artists are generally painters, sculptors, wallpaper hangers, designers, and "aging specialists" (not elderly experts, but people who know how to make a set look like it's about to fall apart). They paint plaster board to look like fine burled walnut paneling, cardboard trees so cleverly that they look capable of photosynthesis; they even paint costumes and make puppets. In addition, they create artwork needed as a prop as long as it's large enough to be considered scenery rather than on-air graphics, which are the graphic artists' bailiwick.

Where to Apply

To become a scenic artist for television, be prepared either to be a general crew member in a small station where you are assigned a variety of tasks, including some scenic design and set painting. Or at a slightly larger station or production house, you may find work as a graphic artist (see Chapter 8.) doing scenic design as well as on-air graphics. Apply to the station or production house's art director.

To work exclusively as a scenic artist, expect to freelance for television stations, production houses, set design shops, and corporate television departments. There are few staff jobs offering employment 52 weeks a year, and those that do are limited mostly to the three networks and major production houses with a heavy program schedule.

As a scenic artist who does only scenic art, your best bet for employment is to become a member and register with the United Scenic Artists Union. When production companies or set production shops are looking for artists, the "Charge Man," the person in charge of the crew working on the production of a particular set, often calls the union and request the names of artists with specific skills. You can also send your resume and try for an appointment to show your portfolio directly to the charge man at set/props production shops.

Set/Scenic/Production Designer

A set/scenic/production designer is not an entry-level position, or even one that can be learned on the job from an entry-level post. As a network senior scenic designer puts it, a scenic designer is "an architect with a dramatic flair." The word *architect* is key here. In addition to their decorative aspects, sets have to be sound structures built according to basic architectural principles.

The scenic designer is responsible for "everything an actor walks on, under, or in between," the designer says. "The designer sets the tone for the whole production's look, supervises the production of the scenery and the staff involved. You have to be an artist, a draftsman, and have taste—good taste."

The set/scenic designer generally reports to the director of the program. As described in Chapter 4, the director is responsible for the overall look of a program. The work of the scenic designer is, therefore, absolutely critical. To get the look the director wants to achieve, the scenic designer must work closely with the costume designer and lighting director.

The aspects of the production for which the designer is responsible include:

- the design and construction of custom furnishings;
- the design and execution of oversized maps, charts and diagrams that are beyond the scope of the station's on-air graphic artists;

- the design and/or acquisition of the components of an interior set—furniture, walls, floors, decor, and accessories;
- the exteriors of buildings for a dramatic show;
- maintenance of sets, scenery, furnishings;
- creation of architectural blue prints that detail the set design including electrical wiring;
- necessary structural and design information;
- supervision of assembly and dismantling of sets.

The scenic designer's job begins with reading the script for a program and coming up with visual ideas for settings appropriate for the mood, time period, and program type. To do so requires not only imagination, but research into the styles of the period and area in which the program is set.

The concepts used by the scenic designer must also be functional—actors must be able to perform on the sets, and the camera must be able to "see" the action. The scenic designer also plans how the set will work in camera shots. To do so, the set designer supplies sketches of the overall set and of different camera shots showing specific compositions from various angles, closeups, and wide shots.

To qualify for scenic design work, it's best to have a four-year degree in art/theater design and as much experience as possible on sets at college, amateur, and regional theater. Work on TV sets for school video or local community television is also an excellent way to get experience. Experience at a scenic production shop that serves networks, advertisers, and film producers is also a good source of training.

Where to Apply

Individuals with staff jobs at the networks report to the director of production services or to an executive with a similar functional title. In smaller settings, the art director of the station or production house may be the person hiring scenic designers (or those who do scenic design in addition to other visually artistic tasks such as graphic design).

For freelance work, it's best to contact the director of a program. Join and register with the United Scenic Artists and with graphic and visual arts associations such as The Art

Directors Club. Once you get started, assuming you are good at what you do, networking generally will take care of you.

Assistant/Associate Technical Director

The position of assistant technical director (ATD) (also known as associate technical director) is not an entry-level position. It exists mainly in network, major production houses and large market stations with sophisticated production equipment and technology.

The assistant technical director's role is two-fold: to assist the technical director by handling certain equipment and to act as substitute technical director. Generally, the assistant technical director's role is to operate special effects equipment that must be coordinated with the technical director's switcher operation.

Corporate television departments usually are not sophisticated enough to have a staff assistant TD (or a full TD for that matter); rather, they tend to rely on an outside production house or freelance production staff for that expertise. The networks often use freelance ATDs, even for established programs.

Where to Apply

See page 52.

Technical Director

The technical director (TD) is responsible for the technical aspects of a production and works closely with the program's director. The director and technical director sit side-by-side in the control room during production.

The TD's principal activity is operation of the switcher, an electronic device that determines which of many camera feeds will actually go on the air or be recorded on tape for later airing. The switcher, which literally switches from one camera output to another, can also create several basic video effects: split screens, fading, dissolving, and superimposition. In some productions, the TD is called the switcher and does nothing but operate the switcher.

"It is important to develop an understanding with the director," notes a network TD. "I basically have to get an understanding of the idea the director has in mind and help create that through the switcher and other visual effects."

Creativity can be an important part of the TD's function, but that depends on the relationship between the TD and the director. "When you get used to your director and communication is good, then you need less direction and your input on the show's look can increase," the network TD says. "You can come up with ideas and suggestions, but a lot depends on your relationship with the director."

If the director doesn't trust the TD or is simply the kind of person who does not like to relinquish control, the TD's job is more technical than creative—a matter of executing commands rather than contributing ideas for what those commands should be.

The TD's responsibilities may also include direction of the crew—the audio engineer, the video engineer, the lighting director, and the camera operator—according to the director's and/or technical manager's instructions, both during pre-production and production. The TD is responsible for setting up facilities and facilities changes that may suddenly occur during production—even during a commercial break!

Technical director positions are not all alike. In some stations, the TD has broad responsibility for the technical aspects of a production. In other stations, the TD's only function is operation of the switcher. In some network situations, where jobs are highly specialized, the position can be limited to technical direction of commercials—inserting the commercials at the appropriate time—or technical direction of on-air promotions that involve simple assembly of prerecorded video and audio.

Where to Apply

In addition to the regular job hunting effort outlined on page 52, call the stations to learn whether TDs are hired for specific programs. If so, you might want to write to the director of the programs. In small stations, the news director may have considerable clout and hiring power for TDs.

Consider freelancing. The networks often use freelance TDs

for news and sports. Major entertainment program production companies also hire freelance TDs for pilots and regular programming.

LIFE AFTER THE CREW: PRODUCING, DIRECTING, AND MANAGING

After you have experienced as many aspects of crew work as possible, you can specialize in one area, such as lighting, cinematography, audio, video, or you can explore different opportunities that bring together several aspects of your experience.

Producer, Co-Producer, Associate/Assistant Producer

An experienced crew member can move into producing. Serious production crew experience can give you an important edge over the aspiring producer who does not have a solid technical background. The same is equally true for directing.

For more information about producing and directing, see Chapter 4.

Production Manager

Full experience as a crew member in several capacities can also qualify you for the position of production manager. A challenging position, the job of production manager involves scheduling production facilities and staff members.

In smaller stations, the production manager has the additional responsibility of hiring producers and directors and other production crew and staff members. To qualify, you need at least three or four years of production experience and considerable interpersonal and managerial skills.

Unit/Manpower/Technical/Operations Manager

In larger stations and production companies, the position of production manager is divided into several jobs: unit manager, manpower manager, technical manager, and operations manager.

The unit manager's responsibilities are primarily logistical and organizational. As a unit manager, you are in charge of the production's budget, scheduling pre-production activities such as set design, equipment setups, etc., and the maintenance and operation of all facilities and equipment.

The manpower/scheduling manager is responsible for scheduling crews and assigning them to different shows and locations. The technical manager assumes the technical responsibilities for a production (or productions) and acts as the liaison between the station or production company's engineering department and the producers and directors of a specific show. Among the technical manager's challenges is keeping the technical level of production as up-to-date as possible.

The operations manager is responsible for the scheduling and smooth operation of the production house or station's production studios, edit rooms, control rooms, and other facilities. The maintenance manager oversees the daily activities of the maintenance engineers, television equipment systems use, and maintenance procedures.

UNIONS

As a television crew person, you can encounter work in both union and nonunion situations. The advantages of a union job include higher salaries, overtime pay (and in television production that can add up to a significant amount of money), special rates for working holidays, and job security (it can be difficult to fire or lay off a member of a strong union).

The main advantage of a nonunion situation is the less rigid definitions of jobs. As a crew member in a nonunion environment you get hands-on experience with a variety of equipment in a variety of capacities. You may find yourself operating video, audio, camera, setting up lights, and working with props—all in one job. Sometimes these duties are simultaneous and sometimes you are audio person on Tuesday and camera operator on Thursday. While being asked to operate audio and video simultaneously can be exhausting, some people find it more interesting over a long term. In the short term it offers a marvelous training opportunity.

You may become a member of a variety of unions—not necessarily the same unions for equivalent jobs in different stations. Except for the field of scenic/set design, joining a union for television production is not difficult; it is automatic when you become employed in a union job. The trick is getting that first union job. There may be an initiation fee, and there are union dues which are usually deducted automatically from your paycheck.

In order to join United Scenic Artists as a set designer, however, you have to pass examinations. You are expected to be able to create complete sets for a production from sketches to blueprints that carpenters and electricians can follow.

Larger stations tend to be unionized; most smaller stations are not. Most public and cable stations, production houses, and corporate television departments are nonunion. Among the unions you might encounter as a crew member are:

- *NABET, National Association of Broadcast Employees and Technicians AFL-CIO:* video and audio engineers, camera operators, lighting directors, technical directors, assistant technical directors, stage managers, second stage managers
- *IBEW, International Brotherhood of Electrical Workers:* video and audio engineers, camera operators, technical directors, assistant technical directors
- *DGA, Directors Guild of America:* technical directors, assistant technical directors, stage managers, second stage managers, unit production managers, production associates
- *United Scenic Artists:* set/scenic designers, scenic artists, art directors, painters, sculptors, costume designers
- *IATSE, International Alliance of Theatrical Stage Employees:* stage hands, scenic designers, property masters, carpenters, lighting people, makeup

FUTURE TRENDS

When we asked crew members what they saw as the future trends in television production, there were two responses that came up over and over again: the professionalization of the television crew and the constant developments of technology.

First, a few words about the new breed of television crew that is developing. The original crew—those who began their careers with the birth of television—included a large proportion of people with little formal education in television. After all, there was no place to get education in television except on the job.

The new breed of television crew is likely to have more formal education in technical areas. Many young television crew people have strong liberal arts backgrounds as well. This follows a trend in which, in many places, crew work is becoming more aesthetically oriented than it has been in the past.

Other changes affecting television production are the constant developments in equipment. With the advent of stereo television and digital audio, audio people have new challenges, not just in working with advancing technology, but in designing sound for a production that makes effective use of that technology.

Continual technological advances in television production equipment are also likely. For example, there is already increased use of computer-enhanced switchers, cameras, audio consoles, and lighting boards. As a result, crew members need to have enough computer background to operate and maintain this equipment. For audio engineers, the development of stereo audio in broadcasting has affected career opportunities. Audio engineers can no longer count on working their way up from office work and learning on the job. Now, because of the increased complexity of television sound systems, technical training and college degrees are required.

With computerization affecting much production equipment, will there be fewer jobs? Not likely, say many television people. The computerized parts of television equipment generally enhance the production quality but don't eliminate the personnel. For example, a computer-registered camera makes the color registration more consistent, but it doesn't substitute for the camera operator.

One issue affecting television crew jobs is whether the networks will produce less in-house and rely more on outside independent production. Some professionals predict that the networks will be producing more in-house in an effort to control production costs and enjoy the profits of lucrative entertainment programming. Either way, the effect on crews will be *where* they work—at networks or production companies—not *whether* they work!

Will there be less crew work in general? Not likely. Television production opportunities are increasing with the growing popularity of television as a communications tool in corporations, the increase of music videos, the boom in home video cassette recorders, and the accompanying demand for educational, exercise, music, and other tapes for home use.

A Talk With . . .

Roger P. Stauss
Freelance Audio Director

> Roger Stauss is a freelance audio director through his own company RPS Location Recording in Fairfield, Connecticut. He has worked on the audio of Kate & Allie, The Merv Griffin Show, *and others, as well as commercials, industrials (corporate television), and sporting events.*

I got my basic audio mixing skills at the University of Hartford where, as a student, I worked for the radio station. I worked for a few years as a radio announcer, disc jockey, reporter. I didn't even want to get near a television studio when I was in radio; but once I got in there, I found it very exciting and that there were a lot more opportunities in television.

I started in television as an intern/volunteer in the production department of the Connecticut Public Television Network (CPTN). I built sets and ran camera and audio. In 1974 I became a part-time staff member, and the following year I began working full time. I served as audio supervisor until I moved to New York City in 1979.

At Connecticut Public Television, I worked on WNET's *Great Performances* and *Theater in America*. I got to know the sound men in those shows. They encouraged me to apply for a job on *Sesame Street* at Reeves Teletape in New York. For a while I was the show's utility person, the technician who puts the mikes on the talent, helps move the cameras around, and makes sure cables are not in the shots. I worked closely with the audio mixer, and when he was on vacation, I assumed his position. Soon afterwards, Reeves re-opened the old Ed Sullivan Theater and made me its full-time audio director.

I like what I do. Every show has its ups and downs, but doing audio for television is a challenge. There are so many different kinds of things you have to consider. I like the challenge of figuring out which mikes go where and how to use them. It's the whole project: seeing it planned, shot, edited and on the air, that's rewarding.

TV technology is changing constantly, so you're always learning. The technology of digital audio and stereo television coming up makes it really exciting.

What would I advise young people? Get as much practical, hands on experience as you can, whether at a trade school or university radio or television station. It's hard to get a job right out of school with no practical experience.

A Talk With . . .

Brad Hagen
Independent Producer/Director/Camera Operator

> *Brad Hagen is owner of Video Resources, a one-man production company located in Irvine, California, that he started in 1980 when he was in his early twenties. Now, Video Resources has clients such as: Procter & Gamble, Sears Roebuck, Philips Medical Systems, Suzuki, J. Walter Thompson, Chiat-Day, and various municipalities. Video Resources' equipment includes an in-house editing system, duplication, broadcast and industrial video cameras and recorders, and assorted sound, lighting, and grip equipment.*

My first job in television was during my last year of junior high school as an instructor's aide in a video production class. I got the job because I had worked with the school's video equipment on some personal projects, had 8-millimeter film-making experience and had experience with photography—I was photographer for the school yearbook. At that time, video equipment was black and white, reel to reel, and the class I worked with involved both field production and some simple editing.

Throughout high school, I took all the courses available in television production, did some freelance photography, and worked as a teacher's aide for some of the television classes.

I went to California State University at Long Beach, where I planned to pursue a degree in business. Then I came across an ad in the newspaper—the Hughes Tool Company was looking for a videotape editor. Armed with the editing experience I'd gained at school, I interviewed for the job and was hired.

I began doing entire productions for the company—eventually developing a department involved in production as well as post-production. At Hughes, I produced between 20 and 40 programs a year. These programs ranged from simple videotapes of engineers presenting technical papers to more complex productions requiring script writers, animation, special effects, distant shooting locations, professional narrators, on-camera talent, and various size crews. I hired the crews and rented equipment either locally or hired them while on location.

I learned a lot on the job. But I also added to my formal education and attended courses on video production and post-production techniques.

In 1979, the oil industry was in a downturn and the activity of my department was decreasing. So, I began doing some freelance work, eventually planning to go into business for myself. My free time was limited, though, so I did only a few freelance industrial productions and a few social—wedding and party—videos. Since I didn't have any equipment of my own at the time, I rented the equipment and hired the freelance crews that I needed.

In 1980 Hughes asked me to transfer to Midland, Texas, and I had to make a choice between working for Hughes in Texas or pursuing my career here in California. I decided to resign from Hughes and stay here and concentrate on making Video Resources a successful company.

For the first eight months after I left Hughes, I did longshore-man and construction work to support myself and Video Resources. But then my video production business began to build rapidly, and I began buying equipment and hiring freelance crews on a regular basis.

I enjoy my work very much because I've been producing so many interesting and challenging video projects. Last year, for example, I shot a commercial for Beatrice [Foods], a product introduction for Warner-Lambert featuring Mike Conners, and a marketing video on a multimillion dollar computer for Infodetics Corporation.

My work is educational in the sense that I work on a variety of projects in so many different industries, from energy to computer sciences to food processing to manufacturing. I also get to work with people who are leaders in their indus-tries and celebrities like Sylvester Stallone and Joan Collins. But I also enjoy the fact that the projects I produce *do* some-thing—they directly contribute to a company's success, or as with a series of safety programs I did, to the safety of employees.

Advice

Of course, I think a balance between formal education and practical experience is necessary. But most important is that you work hard and do the best job you can do no matter how menial. In this business, you also need good common sense, good communication skills, and the ability to work well with people, whether they are your co-workers, your boss, or your client.

A Talk With . . .

Electa Brown
Freelance Associate Director and Stage Manager

> *Electa Brown has been stage manager of the first two seasons of* The Cosby Show, The 1986 Tony Awards, *NBC's 60th Anniversary Special, and* Live Aid—*to name just a few. She has been associate director of* Money World with Adam Smith *(PBS),* Hallmark

Hall of Fame, various specials, and a lot of sports.
Brown has also directed remotes for WNET shows. She
has won Directors Guild of America awards for her work
on The Cosby Show *and* Motown Returns to the
Apollo.

I got my BFA in TV and film at NYU. The first year there, I spent a lot of time editing film with a moviola—lonely and laborious work. Then, one day I went to pick up a friend at the TV Control Room and was amazed! I watched them "edit" with four images in front of them at the same time. With a moviola, you only work with one image at a time. That's how I got hooked on TV—it was the immediacy, the instant gratification.

It took me a long time to break into TV and get into the DGA [Directors Guild of America]. I had my dream—to direct live theater for TV—when I was 23. I didn't get my break until I was 33.

I spent a year and a half at NBC trying to get an associate director job through Personnel. Finally, I handed a production head my resume, which he hardly looked at. He asked me what I thought the best East Coast TV school is. I thought, "NYU." He said, "NYU." I said, "I went there," which made him look at my resume again. He then noticed that I have a pilot's license, and we started talking about flying. Finally, he said, "If you can fly a plane, you can be an AD!" But the job wasn't in the bag. I called him every week for seven months before I got my break with NBC as a vacation relief AD.

After a season with NBC, I went freelance as an AD. Along the way, someone said that there was a stage manager's job available for a two-week industrial. I called a few friends and asked them how to stage manage and talked my way into the job.

It's real hard work to get started, but, God, I love it. Some of the opportunities I've had, I would have paid for. Imagine getting paid to work on *Motown Returns to the Apollo, The Cosby Show, Live Aid,* or live sporting events. I still work at Shea from time to time, as well as with NBC network and WOR sports.

Advice

Learn to type. Take any job, any place, anywhere. You can't expect to work or make any real money right away. I spent ten years trying to get into TV, and then spent six years working all kinds of hours—TV is a 24-hour business. People say to me: "It looks like you have a really neat job. I'd like to do that." And I answer, "Do you want to make plans with your life? Do you want to have any kind of love life? If you do, you can forget about the freelance life. But, oh, the rewards are great—if you stick it out."

A Talk With . . .

Norm Davidson
Senior Scenic Designer, NBC-TV

> *Norm Davidson has worked in television scenic design for over 30 years. A graduate of the Yale School of Drama, he has been on the interviewing committee for the United Scenic Artists, the union representing scenic and set designers and other theatrical crafts people for theater, movie and television production.*

A lot of us in television scenic design have strange and checkered careers. Ninety-five percent of us—at least of the older generation of which I'm a member—are theater trained. I started working in the theater at the age of twelve in the Borscht Belt [New York's Catskill Mountain area resorts]. I used to help paint scenery, and I even acted as a stooge sometimes if a comedian needed one. I didn't get paid—this was during the depression, and I did it for the free food and the fresh air.

As a scenic designer, I'm basically an architect with dramatic flair. I'm also a jack of all trades. I've been an actor, a director, and a painter. Experience as a director has helped me a lot, because I understand what a director needs.

The work situation in television scenic design has changed a lot over the years. When I began at NBC, we had 35 full-time staff scenic designers. Today we only have three and the rest are per-diem freelancers. The reason is that the networks don't produce so much of their own programming any more.

Today, most of the jobs for scenic designers are freelance, so it's good to be able to design for theater, television, and film.

Do I like what I do? I've been doing it for over 30 years; that should answer your question! It's fun. You have to work hard to be bored: Every day there is something different. If you have to do the same thing every day you might as well be a robot. The moment I get bored, I'll leave.

Advice

You have to be versatile. You can't just do one style such as drama, or comedy. If you do, you'll starve to death . . .

The best teacher is actual experience. My advice to young people just coming out of school is to get a job in a set production shop. You'll get practical experience executing design.

When you design you work with a delicate brush with two hairs. When you execute, you paint with a four-inch brush. Try painting a tree that way, try painting the foliage and having it look real. You've got to get your hands dirty and lug a five-gallon bucket of paint up a ladder. When you interview for a job, don't come in with a snobby attitude. Show you're not afraid to get your hands dirty.

Don't use computer-aided design too much; don't let it become a crutch. You have to be able to draw with a pencil, not just a machine. Computers are a good tool, but it's crazy to rely on it. Remember, the basis of this business is imagination.

A Talk With . . .

Katie McGuire
News Videographer (Camera Operator) and
Editor, WTEN, Albany, New York

> *WTEN is the ABC affiliate in Albany, New York, which is in the 50th market. McGuire is responsible both for shooting and editing news footage for WTEN's daily news programs and documentaries. As an editor, McGuire doesn't just supervise a tape editor, she physically edits the stories, the graphics, promotional spots, teasers, and bumpers. As a mass communications major*

*at the University of Vermont, she got significant hands-on
television and film production experience —editing, producing, directing, writing, and camera work.*

After I graduated, I applied for a job as a television editor in
Burlington, Vermont. They were actually looking for a man—
this was in 1973—because they wanted someone who would
eventually go out and shoot stories. They thought only a man
could carry heavy equipment. It took me a couple of weeks to
convince them that I was capable of doing the work. They
finally hired me as a film editor—they were shooting black
and white film then.

I wasn't working for them very long before I started shooting
sports events and then news. I spent three years in Burlington, and then I wanted to work in a larger market, so I came to
Albany where I've been since 1976.

Shooting news and shooting sports actually have a lot in common. If you miss a touchdown in football, they aren't going to
play it again for you. It's the same in news. You only get one
chance to cover the event. You always have to be prepared
and alert. You have to listen, think visually, and if a person
talks about a lot of different things in an interview, think of
ways to show it on camera and then remember to do it.

I like what I do. It's exciting. There's always something different. I get to do a lot of things you normally don't get to do. For
example, I spent ten days in Moscow in January 1986 covering
the Empire State Institute for the Performing Arts' visit under
the first Reagan-Gorbachev cultural exchanges. They sent
only a reporter and me . . . The two of us produced a four-
part series on the city of Moscow, a five-part series on the
troupe itself, and then one half-hour show. It was an incredible amount of work—we averaged three or four hours of
sleep a night. But it was exciting being part of the exchange.

On the negative side, there are days when you may not be
assigned to exciting stories. You just don't get exciting stories
every day, but being able to cover something like Moscow
makes up for that.

Advice

Get all the experience you can, whether it be in school, doing
internships—whatever you can get. And ask questions. I find

that most students who come and intern here don't want to ask questions. I think sometimes they are awed and that's why they don't ask.

Also, you have to be prepared to do a lot of work—nights and weekends. Television news is not a nine-to-five job. When they call you in the middle of the night and tell you there's a fire or an accident to cover, you have to be ready to go.

A Talk With . . .

Judy Seabridge
Production Manager, WTEN, Albany, New York

> *As production manager of WTEN, an ABC affiliate in the 50th market, Judy Seabridge reports to the station's general manager and is responsible for scheduling facilities and crews for the station's own productions. In addition to her managerial work, Seabridge, a former producer/ director, also continues to produce and direct special programs for the station.*

My first job in television was as a producer/director in 1975 here at WTEN. It was a complete fluke to be hired in such a responsible position just starting in the business. I had just gotten a masters degree in educational communications and canvassed all the local television stations looking for an entry-level job in TV. WTEN had just lost a director and was looking for a replacement and was willing to train—mostly because they weren't able to pay a lot for the position. I had some experience directing as part of a television production course for my masters; each student got to be part of the crew on other student's projects, so I had minimal experience with each production job.

I managed to convince them I was trainable, and once I was hired, I was immediately trained to direct the news. For weeks, I sat side by side with one of the news directors and learned to call and compose shots, and since directors here do their own technical directing, I was also pushing buttons [operating the switcher].

Once I became fully trained on news, I was eased into working on commercial production, both directing and producing television commercials for local advertisers. For that I had to learn how to put things together properly. There are many approaches to getting the final spot on tape. My job was to do it most efficiently and cost effectively for the client.

[Before becoming production manager at WTEN, Judy did a stint at the Albany public television station as a producer/director.] I had worked on what was loosely called cultural affairs programming. That involved mostly taping music performances. I directed a series of performances of the Albany Symphony Orchestra, produced and directed the premiere performance of the Empire State Youth Orchestra, and I worked on the two-day Newport Jazz Festival in Saratoga, which was eventually edited into an eight-part series of jazz specials. That kind of work broadened my directing experience. It's very demanding work, having the cameras on drums when the drums come in, capturing flutes when the flutes come in, keeping up with the music, getting a person to read the scores and to make sure we were pacing and cutting properly.

What do I like about being production manager? I like being a manager of people and finding ways to raise the standard of performance and quality of the people who are working for me and other departments. At the production end of things you need someone who can ask you to stretch yourself a bit more and make the picture in every frame better composed, better presented, and better paced. I think that's the challenge for the production manager.

Being a production manager at a local station in particular is a nice position because you have the opportunity to offer expertise in more than just your own department. You can be a part of news, part of planning for the whole station, part of special projects. Here I continue to produce and direct. I haven't given up doing production by becoming a manager of the process.

4

Producers and Directors

Put ten television producers or directors in one room and ask each one how to become a producer or a director. You'll get ten different answers.

Producers and directors come from a variety of different backgrounds, disciplines, and even industries. Their roles range from hands-on to purely titular, and their starts in the business may have been haphazard, calculated, hard-won, or nepotistic.

The *producer* of a television show is the person with the overall responsibility for a program—from concept through the final edit, from budget through casting, sets, and location. Often the producer is the person who came up with the original idea for the program.

A producer may do more than just produce. Sometimes the producer is a producer-writer (or writer-producer) and writes the script. Sometimes the producer also hosts the show (as producer-correspondent or producer-host) and sometimes directs it (as producer-director).

A *director* is the person responsible for the "look" and technical quality of the program. The director's responsibilities include the camera angles, framing, sequences and pacing, the lighting, the sets, the audio, the video, the acting or performances of the actors or "talent." Ideally the director should be involved in a program from the beginning, but sometimes the director steps in just before shooting.

While producers and directors have different roles, the essential qualities required for either are the same with the exception that the director must understand the technical aspects of production while the producer should, but need not.

WHAT THE PRODUCER AND DIRECTOR DO ———

A producer or director, whether on a network series or a local cable interview show, is involved in the total program. Ideally, the director can cover for any weaknesses in the crew and correct errors.

If you are the producer or director, you do not have to know how to operate a camera, set up lighting, or work an editing machine, but you should know what these tools do. You must know what a good picture looks like when you look at the monitor and what kinds of changes are possible to improve on it.

Producing and directing, although distinctly different functions, have a lot in common. A producer or a director must be a good manager, know what needs to be accomplished and be able to delegate that responsibility to staff or crew. There are three essentials to being a good manager:

1. *The willingness and ability to delegate responsibility.* You can delegate responsibility when you trust people to do their job properly. Therefore, being a good manager means *recognizing talent,* and either working with it, or working around it. (You don't always get to handpick your crew, and the ability to make the best of what you've got is critical.)

2. *The ability to communicate and be friendly at the same time.* If you can't tell people what you want in a friendly, constructive way, chances are they won't listen. "Television is teamwork and if you get just one member of the team angry, the whole team suffers," notes one network associate director.

3. *A well-organized and attentive personality.* Television production involves many processes performed by many people. There is little room for mistakes. Both the producer and the director are responsible for the smooth running of a production, and that means being organized and on top of the many details involved.

From "Indy Prod" to Network

As a producer or director, you can work on staff at a network, public, local or cable television station, a production company or in a corporate television department. Or you can freelance, in which case you'll be known as an "indy" or independent producer (indy prod) or independent director. There are many differences between going solo as an independent and working on staff. First, as a staff producer, you have to work within a budget, but you don't have to raise the money that backs up your budget; as an independent producer, you are responsible for raising the money for your program.

As a staff producer or director, you will be assigned programs. As a freelancer, you are not limited to the shows produced by a particular company. On the other hand, as a freelancer, until you hit the big time you may find yourself taking whatever you can get, which can include programs you don't like and/or have little respect for.

A staff director or producer may have little choice in the crew members assigned to the show. An independent producer and director can handpick the crew.

Which course you choose to pursue depends on your talent, personality, preferences, and on luck.

A DAY WITH PRODUCERS AND DIRECTORS

The nature of a producer or director's day depends on the schedule for that day. Is it a day when you'll be taping a program? Is it a day when you'll be locked up in an editing room for a lot longer than a "day"? Or are you still in the stage that occupies most of your producing or directing time—preproduction planning?

There's a difference between producing and directing live programs and taped ones. When you are working live every day (as in news and sports), your pre-production planning is routine. As producer or director you must round up what crew members you need and assign them their jobs.

When you are working live on a special presentation, such as a European summit meeting between heads of state, or the summer Olympics, or a live musical or entertainment broadcast, you have weeks or even months of pre-production planning behind you.

Planning includes determining how many cameras you need, scouting the location, taking stock of the studio to ascertain what kind of movements the cameras can make, finding out what kind of lighting you need, and working out strategies.

Pre-production planning also involves the producer and director working together (ideally) to decide where the talent should be, how the scenes will be shot (if it's a scripted program such as an entertainment special, drama, or comedy), where you want closeups, where you want to pan, etc. You should create lists of all equipment and props that will be necessary during the taping, and see to it that all items are procured and in their place before the taping.

These are only *some* of the possible items on the pre-planning agenda for producers and directors, but they give an idea of the scope of the two jobs. Three sample days spent with two different producers and one news director follow.

A Day With . . .
An *Evening Magazine* Program Producer

There are several kinds of producers involved with the production of Evening Magazine, the program known in some markets as PM magazine. At the top is the program producer in charge of the entire show. Next in command is the associate program producer, who acts as backup and right arm to the program producer. There are also field producers who write the scripts for the show's sequences and produce them.

There is also a wraps producer responsible for the studio-taped segments which include the opening and closing of the show that "wrap up" the program, the introductions to stories that were shot outside the studio by field producers, and the chatter that leads into and back from commercials.

Evening Magazine is produced five times a week. As a cooperative television production, the individual stations

that run the show produce some but not all the seg-
ments that they air. What each station produces goes
into a pool accessible to the other stations as well as the
one producing it.

Each station airing Evening Magazine *has its own pair*
of hosts. Therefore a station cannot run segments as they
come in from the national pool but must tape its own
segments with hosts' reading the voiceovers. In addition,
the program producer may want to adapt a national story
for the station's market by finding a local angle and ei-
ther shooting or scripting additional material.

7 AM

The program producer arrives to observe the final mix and
edit of the evening's show. This process begins at about 6:30
AM and runs until about 9 AM.

9:30 AM–5 PM (or later)

The evening's program ready to go, the program producer
continues the daily and day-long process of choosing stories
for shows to come. This process involves:

- Selecting stories from newspapers, magazines, press releases, and other information sources for possible production by the field producers.
- Screening the "national reel" for possible stories. The national reel, which arrives once a week, is a selection of
  stories produced by other *Evening Magazine* stations in the
  cooperative.
- Approving scripts for segments about to be produced.
- Screening locally-produced stories.
- Advising field producers: providing them with direction,
  finding themes, recommending approaches, and suggestions for people to be interviewed.

A Day With . . .
An Associate Producer for a Live Daily Talk Show

This associate producer works for People Are Talking, *a*
live daily talk show broadcast by KYW-TV in Philadelphia,
which is in the fourth market. Like Donahue, *the show*

*focuses on one subject, has a large studio audience,
and takes in viewer phone calls. It airs daily from 10 AM
to 11 AM.*

*The staff includes a program producer with overall re-
sponsibility for all shows produced, a coordinating producer who backs up the program producer and produces
two shows a week, and two associate producers who
alternate shows.*

*The show producers (the coordinating producer and
the associate producers) are responsible for ideas for
their shows, booking guests, pre-interviewing the guests,
and writing scripts for the program's hosts, as well as supervising the show during airtime.*

8 AM

The show's associate producer arrives. If there is something
complicated in the show, such as a cooking demonstration or
a vignette with actors, the producer comes in earlier.

From 8 to 8:45, the associate producer transfers any pre-
taped segments to a single tape for airing. Pre-taped segments
might be a series of scenes from an actor's screen career or
news footage pertaining to a program's guest.

8:45 AM

Meeting of director, associate producer, program producer,
audio person, camera operator, lighting director, stage manager. The associate producer has created a show format—a
printed schedule on a sheet of legal-size paper. The format
lists the topic, who will be interviewed, the additional audio
or video clips that will be used, at what time and for how long
and in what order. Everybody goes down the show's schedule
to make sure they all understand the plan.

9:15 AM

Guests arrive by 9:15. They come into the Green Room, a
theater-derived term for the guest reception room which is
seldom green. An intern usually staffs the room, has the
guests fill out the appropriate release and information forms.
The associate producer talks to the guests briefly, goes over
the show's schedules and tries to keep them from talking too
much before the show to keep their material fresh for the
actual broadcast.

9:50 AM

Associate producer brings the first guests into the studio.

10 AM

The live show begins. While the show is airing, the associate producer, who stays on the set, wears an audio headset that connects to the program producer, who is in the control room. (The associate producer is called the line producer when working on the studio floor.) The program producer gives instructions and advice to the associate producer through the headset.

The associate producer has a series of blank cue cards and a heavy marker on hand throughout the show for writing messages to the on-camera hosts: "Take a viewer phone call." "Take a question from the audience." "Challenge what that guest just said." Union rules dictate that the associate producer hand the cue cards to the stage manager who is the one who flashes them at the show's host.

During commercial breaks, the associate producer goes over the show schedule and notes any necessary changes. Obviously, on a live show, it's absolutely essential to stay on top of things. Changes might include finding a new spot for a topic that was accidentally skipped over and replaced by one planned for later in the show. Or if more than the allotted time was devoted to one subject, a topic must be eliminated from the remainder of the show so that the program can still end on time.

11 AM

The show is off the air.

11:15 AM

If the associate producer is line-producing the next morning's show, he or she will say quick goodbyes and thanks to the guests and return to the studio to record promotional spots with the host for the upcoming show.

11:45 AM

The associate producer returns to the office and reorganizes the folder containing all the notes and script material for the show just produced. Work begins on the next day's show. The work on any given afternoon could include any and all of the following:

- Trying to locate appropriate guests and experts. Some shows, such as ABC network's *Good Morning America*, have their own bookers who take care of this process. Others, such as Group W Broadcasting owned stations, share a central booking office that helps with some of the booking.
- Pre-interviews of possible guests. This involves interviewing the potential guests on the telephone and selecting the key questions and the key responses that will be covered in the actual show.
- Transcribing the audiotapes of the pre-interviews.
- Writing scripts for guest interviews. The associate producer writes the key questions the host will ask (and read from the teleprompter) and outlines the guest response.
- Writing promos—the spots in which the program's host will announce the next show's topics.
- Research. Doing research on the topic of a program. Assigning an intern to do research in the book and magazine or tape library.
- Assembling props. Gathering all the props necessary for an upcoming show.
- Updating the program producer. Discussing status of various programs being developed, new ideas, etc.

4 PM

Production meeting with the program producer, line producer, and the host regarding the next day's program. Reviewing the scripts with the host and making any necessary stylistic or other changes.

4:30 PM

If producing the next day's show, the associate producer will organize the paperwork for the next morning, gather the music and any videotaped footage that may be needed. Otherwise, he or she takes care of various odds and ends and goes home.

A Day With . . .

A Cable TV News Director

The news director heads a news program on a major market cable station. The show airs weeknights (Monday through Friday) in the early evening. It is 30 minutes long. In this particular case the news director triples as the anchor person and the executive producer. The staff consists of six reporter/field producers, six camera operator/editors, one program producer, one assignment editor, one sports director, one part-time weather person, and a part-time secretary.

The news director's job goes beyond the actual production of the news program. It is a management position as well, and the news director may spend several hours a day at management meetings held by the station's owner, interview job candidates, and complete the miscellaneous paperwork associated with most management positions in any business. In the news director's absence, the program producer acts as news director.

6 AM

The assignment editor arrives and goes over the news stories already assigned for that day and checks the wire services for news of other stories that may preempt some of the assigned ones.

7 AM–9 AM

Before leaving home, the news director listens to a news radio channel and scans the morning paper. The news director arrives somewhere between 7 and 9 AM, depending on how hectic the day is. Top breaking stories, such as an international hijacking, a major war breaking out, or a natural disaster, require an earlier arrival. Upon arrival, the news director tells the assignment editor of anything unusual heard on the radio on the way in. Usually it's not news to the assignment editor, but occasionally it is.

Reporters arrive according to a staggered schedule. Some come in at 7:30, others at 8:30, and the latest at 9 AM. They begin their phone work to set up stories they are working on that day. They call places they are planning to go, people they are planning to interview, etc.

9 AM

The news director, program producer, and assignment editor go over the assignment board containing lists of all the stories for that evening's show.

9:15 AM

The program producer is dispatched to begin pulling whatever file footage will be necessary for the stories planned for the show. The program producer also writes some of the stories, the teasers (for example, "Rabbits take over the Senate, when the evening news returns in a moment"), and writes the program schedule with a complete rundown of all planned stories.

10–11 AM

The camera operators begin coming in. The producer or news director writes the script for a minute-and-a-half news headline spot to be aired at noon.

11 AM

Most field production teams are out of the studio on assignment.

Noon

The anchorperson/news director appears on camera for a live minute-and-a-half news headline report.

3 PM

Scripts begin to come in from the field producers. The video editing begins now, too. The news director and program producer review the scripts. The news director, who in this case is also the anchor, rewrites some of the scripts, tightens others.

4 PM

Most stories are in by now, written and edited. Others will still be in the editing process until shortly before air time at 5 PM. The news director reviews all stories (if possible) before air time.

5 PM

Air time.

5:45 PM–As Long as It Takes

News director, assignment editor, and program producer begin to review advance stories and news assignments scheduled for the next day's program.

CAREER PATH FOR PRODUCERS AND DIRECTORS

The career path for producing and directing is somewhat parallel. Essentially, both jobs require the ability to oversee a production, though from slightly different perspectives.

The producer has total responsibility for the program from writing to the final edit. In contrast, the director generally is responsible for making sure the final tape contains everything the editor will need to pull the program together.

While it is the director who is responsible for the work of the entire crew, the producer is responsible for the work of the director (and by extension, the crew as well). The principal difference between the two positions in terms of training is technical.

Because of the overlap of the two positions, you will find that many producers were once directors and vice versa. Often the roles are merged, and professionals are producer-directors of their programs.

Network versus Small Operation

In the 1970s and early 1980s, joining one of the networks as a production assistant, a page, or a secretary was a good way to start. There were new programs starting up and people switching from network to network. An entry-level person could hope to move up the ranks within two or three years. In the mid-80s however, there have been many personnel cutbacks, at CBS and ABC in particular, and upward mobility has been greatly reduced.

The conventional wisdom today is that you are best off
starting your producing or directing career in a small station,
small production house, or a corporate television department.
You will generally get more hands-on opportunities in many
different functions. This all-round television production training, which is only possible in a small nonunion environment,
is invaluable.

For both producing and directing, the career paths begin
the same way whether in entertainment or news. Even after the
paths have diverged, there is crossover between news and entertainment (and even advertising), with people from all sides
respecting the special gifts and training acquired in different
places. However, as soon as you know what kind of programming is your ideal line of work, try to get into it.

For information about entry-level jobs see Chapter 2.

Readers (Entertainment)

"It's the one intellectual job in television you can get without
having any production experience," says a producer who got
her start reading for HBO in California. Often a freelance, but
also a part-time or full-time staff position, being a reader is an
ideal entree into television production work. As a reader, your
responsibility is to read unsolicited manuscripts that are sent
in to major television studios, the pay cable enterprises that
produce some of their own programming (HBO and Showtime, for example), and the large production houses (such as
Lorimar, MTM Productions, and others). Generally the manuscripts are for new series (comedy, drama), specials (entertainment), and made-for-television movies.

Readers provide a brief report that includes a log line (brief
factual description of a story including the setting and central
character and central dramatic situation) and a concept line (a
brief description of the point of the story, or the moral of the
story as in "a coming of age story in which three young men
travel through . . .").

"What you have to do," said Dorothy Gilbert, director of
development, Daniel Wilson Productions during a "Young
Professionals Seminar" sponsored by New York Women in
Film, "is to get some reading samples. That means just go and

read, read two books and read two screenplays and write up synopses."

Where to Apply

Contact the major studios, premium cable television services (HBO and Showtime), and entertainment production companies to find out the name of the story editor of a specific program, or the head of program development. Send a cover letter, your reader samples, and your resume.

Copy Person (News and Sports)

An entry-level position ideal for those whose career objectives are news producing or directing. Basic responsibilities include tearing copy off the wire machines (Associated Press, Reuters, and other news services send news stories through machines that print them out automatically), delivering copy and scripts throughout the news room, getting coffee, delivering materials. Basically this is a "gofer" position.

Where to Apply

Apply individually to the news directors of all news shows at each station (cable, local, network) where you would like to work.

Desk Assistant (News and Sports)

An entry-level position in some places, the next step up from copy person in others. An ideal opportunity for the person whose career goal is to become a news or sports producer or director. A desk assistant handles phones and takes messages in addition to copy-person type responsibilities. At the networks, a desk assistant applicant may have to pass a writing test to qualify for the position.

Where to Apply

Apply to the news or sports director of each news or sports show at each station (cable, local and network) where you are interested in working. Switching from sports to news and vice versa, is common. If you can get a job in one area but would prefer the other, don't worry about it. The skills you develop in news and sports production are very similar. The deadline pressures are the same, and both involve live broadcasting and coverage of an event that only happens once (there are no rehearsals in news and sports events) and, therefore, must be done right the first time.

Production Assistant

For general information regarding the position of production assistant, see Chapter 2. Aspiring producers and directors should note the importance a production assistant (PA) job can play in their career. One network producer said when she hires she looks for writing, research, and organizational skills because "a PA is a producer in the making."

Aspiring directors may want to look for a job as a PA assigned to the associate director. This is a perfect spot for learning how to direct. At the networks, where much hiring is done from within, such a production assistant often has a good chance of becoming the assistant news director.

Assignment Editor (News and Sports)

A very demanding, high-pressure job and a good launching spot for a career in news or sports as a reporter, producer, or director. Previous experience usually needed is assignment editing for a smaller station than the one to which you are applying or assignment editing for a radio news program. In smaller stations, you can be promoted to assignment editor from desk assistant or production assistant if you manage to receive the appropriate training.

The assignment editor is responsible for assigning crews and reporters to cover stories. That brief description may make the job sound tame; it is anything but. You have to be on top of the news not only to know what is newsworthy, but to anticipate the news and have your crews available and in the right place at the right time. "You have to be close to clairvoyant," says a former network assignment editor. "If you don't assign a crew to what turns out to be a big story, you are blamed. If you choose to cover the right story, the producer gets the praise. It's a tough and thankless job, but its an important one." The job is one of logistics and organization.

As the network assignment editor says, ". . . sometimes the most important focus of the job is not having good news sense—choosing the most newsworthy story—but covering whatever the other networks or competing stations are covering. That factor can make the post of assignment editor politically volatile."

In network there are many assignment editor posts, both foreign posts and several domestic posts (each editor assigned to different regions of the United States). In local news and even cable network news, there may be only one assignment editor for a news show.

Where to Apply
Write to the news director of as many news programs at as many stations as you possibly can.

Writer
For detailed information about television writing, see Chapter 5. Writing can often lead to producing and directing. Newswriting positions can often lead to studio and field news producing because often, especially in smaller stations, producers are responsible for writing scripts themselves. If not, they are at least responsible for determining the quality of scripts and rewriting them where necessary. Therefore it helps to have experience as a writer. Entertainment writers also may become producers because as producers they have more control over the final production of their stories.

Associate Producer
An associate producer begins as an apprentice producer but functions as a producer once fully trained. Production assistants and writers, especially those who have had the opportunity to co-produce programs, often qualify for promotion into this position. (For more information about this position, see "A day with . . . " on pages 87–90.)

Where to Apply

Apply to the program producer or news director of the specific shows.

Field Producer/Segment Producer ────────────────

A field producer is responsible for putting together stories that are shot outside the studio on location. A segment producer is responsible for producing an entire segment of a broadcast program, such as CBS's *Sixty Minutes*, ABC's *20/20*, or NBC's *1986*. In private television, the equivalent is a corporate news video.

News stories shot where they are happening (at the site of the press conference, on the battlefield) are considered field productions or "remote shoots," as are segments for magazine-style shows such as interviews for *Entertainment Tonight* or for *20/20*.

In smaller stations the field producer may also triple as the on-air reporter and script writer and may produce as many as five to ten complete stories in one work day. At the network level, the field producer works with a reporter and probably produces no more than one story a day.

ABC executive and author Av Westin tells what a field producer does in his book, *Newswatch: How TV Decides the News* (Simon and Schuster, 1982): "The field producer straddles the editorial and technical sides involved in getting a story on the air." He goes on to say that field producers must be good reporters and writers with an extra dash of logistical and organizational skills. Among the field producer's responsibilities are getting the story, supervising the camera crew, locating the telephone lines and necessary electric power outlets, and, as Westin points out, even making sure that the crew has escape routes in crowds.

Where to Apply

For broadcast and cable jobs, apply to the program producer or news director of individual shows. For a private television job, apply to the director or manager of the video department of a corporation or other producing entity. Contact your local chapter of the International Television Association (ITVA) for information about private television opportunities near you.

Associate Director

This is not an entry-level job. An associate director (AD) must have several years of production experience before getting on-the-job training. Technically, an AD is an assistant to the director (in film, this position is called "assistant director,") and as such, the AD's responsibility is to prepare everything for the director.

What an AD actually does depends on the type of program and the personality of the director. Often stage managing experience can qualify you for directing; see Chapter 3. In sports coverage, an AD may act like a stage manager cueing the announcer, keeping one eye on the clock and the other eye on the sports action (often with a pair of binoculars) to let the director know of anything the camera operators should be following. In a delayed broadcast, the AD keeps detailed notes on the action in order to cue the announcers appropriately. As one AD who has handled a lot of sports puts it: "My responsibility is to make sure things run smoothly so that the director can do his or her job—select the camera shots and angles."

As an AD for an edit session, you might be another pair of eyes to make sure there are no oversights or mistakes; your input may be a significant component of the edit session. As an AD on master control for a noncomputerized broadcast, you may perform a job worthy of the juggling skills of the Flying Karamazov Brothers. Since you are responsible for what physically is on the air during your shift, you are coordinating the announcer, the tape room, the film room, the Chyron (titles) inserts, while making sure the right programs, commercials, promos, and station IDs (with the appropriate audio) all go on the air at the right time. No doubt you've seen what happens when master control gets out of control: *Gilligan's Island* runs with the audio of a Coca Cola commercial, or there are long spans of seconds with no picture and no audio.

In studio shooting for entertainment and news programs, the AD sits in the control booth with the director and prepares the camera operators for the shots the director has indicated on the final shooting script. When the director says, "Camera 2," Camera 2 will be focused and ready where the director wants. The AD's function may be to execute the director's orders, or it may be more creative depending on the relationship between the two people.

During rehearsal the AD often takes detailed notes of specific camera movements which the director selects. If one of these selections works well, the AD helps the director recall them for the final taping.

If it is a creative and trusting relationship, the AD and the director will work together in terms of planning the camera work, lighting, and audio effects.

Where to Apply

AD jobs are available both freelance and full-time. Generally, apply to the directors of specific programs that interest you. An excellent way to find out the person to contact is to call the Directors Guild of America. They maintain an updated list, appropriately entitled "People Who Hire," with the names of contacts at the networks and local stations. (See the Appendix for the address of the DGA.)

You can also call the station or production company that produces a show and ask for the directors' names. Or watch the programs and copy down their names from the screen credits at the beginning or end of the show.

If you have no experience yet as an AD, your best bet is to become a production assistant or crew member (see Chapter 3) at a station or production company where you would have the opportunity to observe a director. Try to get to work directly for the director and become an AD. New ADs at the networks and major market stations are usually promotions from within. Corporate television departments generally aren't large enough to hire a full-time associate director.

Director

The director is responsible for the performance of the talent and all members of the technical crew. In news, the position of director is distinct from *news director*; the latter plays a role quite similar to that of executive producer (see page 102), managing the overall production of the show.

An example of what a director does: At a morning news show where four cameras are being used to shoot a live performance of a visiting children's chorus, the director, sitting in the control room, talks over the private line to the four camera operators and gives instructions about what to focus on: "Camera 4, close-up of faces; Camera 2, pan left . . ." The director then selects a shot and tells the technical director which camera should go on air. In addition, the director is responsible for telling the technical director to create visual effects such as fading, dissolving, and superimposing. Finally, the director oversees the lighting and the performances.

The job is something like that of an orchestra conductor. The director follows the script (score) and directs (conducts) the various crew members (orchestra) and talent (soloists) to help interpret the producer's (composer's) vision.

In network and for major independent productions, directing is a high-level, high-pressure job. In smaller television productions, such as cable, local, and private/corporate television, the directing and producing functions may be combined.

In freelancing, many producers and directors double as producer-directors. However, as a freelance director (and not a producer), you may find yourself stepping into production only for the day of taping.

Where to Apply

Apply to the program producer or executive producer of television shows that interest you. To find out names of people hiring directors, contact the Directors Guild of America for their list of "People Who Hire."

In smaller markets, apply for a producing/directing position since budgets may not be able to handle the luxury of a director who only directs. In private television, apply to the managers of corporate television/video departments, who may be eager to use your services for shooting days although tight budgets prevent most from being able to hire directors from the start.

Program Producer/Producer

The program producer, also known simply as the producer, is responsible for all shows produced in a series, or the overall production of a segmented show, or a single show if it is a one-shot special. This means the program producer oversees the field producers, studio producers, associate producers, line producers, director, and all other staff.

Where to Apply

Job opportunities exist at the networks, at local station productions, at independent production houses, and in corporate/private television.

In network, independent production, and local station production, apply to the executive producer of the shows that interest you. In corporate/private television, apply to the manager (often a vice president) of the video/television department.

Executive Producer

The function of executive producer in television ranges from a hands-on producing role to an administrative corporate role depending on the people, the situation, the politics, and the financial structure. As an executive producer, you will have arrived at the business level of television production where ratings, revenues, and the bottom line all count as much as creativity and vision.

In entertainment, executive producers oversee a variety of serial programs sold to the major networks. Executive producers who manage several programs can act either as marketing/packaging executives, creative professionals, or both. Aaron Spelling is typical of an executive producer who combines both marketing savvy and creative vision. His personal style and stamp are evident in his very successful productions including *Fantasy Island, Love Boat,* and *Dynasty.*

In news, an executive producer may act as the video equivalent of an editor-in-chief, reviewing and approving every news story and the entire news program every day. The news executive producer is also likely to have the final say on all hiring for the program.

In corporate television, the executive producer may be an executive in marketing or public relations. In this case, the executive producer may be responsible for the decision to make video programs, review all scripts before production, and review rough cuts of shows before they enter the costly on-line edit stage. The corporate executive producer is unlikely to have hands-on experience with television or video and may simply act as a rubber stamp in hiring. However, as corporate/private television comes of age, the executive producer will become more savvy. Within the next ten years, video and television training may even become a prerequisite for the communications executive.

While producers and directors can be typecast—"He only does game shows; she's only good for documentaries"—you can apply your ability to produce or direct many different kinds of shows. Think about the kinds of programs you like to watch. Those are generally the kind you will enjoy producing or directing.

UNIONS

As you work toward a career as a producer and/or director, you will probably encounter a variety of unions representing the jobs you hold along the way. Membership is usually automatic with your employment and only requires the payment of an initiation fee and monthly or yearly dues all of which are deducted from your paycheck.

As a rule, expect unions in larger markets, and few unions for jobs in smaller markets. Also, expect no uniformity about which union a particular position will be covered by in various larger market stations. Union jurisdiction is a political issue and is resolved differently in different places.

As a freelance or full-time staff producer or a director at some major market stations or as part of a large production house, you may be a member of the Writers Guild of America

(WGA) or the Directors Guild of America (DGA), respectively. Both the WGA and the DGA function in similar ways. Production companies, studios, and networks who are signatories of the WGA or DGA, can hire only Guild members and must adhere to the Guild contract in terms of payment, credits, job responsibilities, rights regarding syndication of a program, number of air times, creative control, etc.

If you are a member of a Guild, you can work only for signatories. You can get a Guild-represented job without being a member, but you have to join the Guild within a specified length of time. In addition to providing minimum pay scales, the Guilds also provide pension funds and life and health insurance—even for freelancers.

A partial list of job positions and the possible unions you might encounter follows.

Interns: Unpaid positions, not represented by any union.

Production Assistants: National Association of Broadcast Employees and Technicians, AFL-CIO (NABET), Directors Guild of America (DGA).

Researchers: NABET or Writers Guild of America (WGA).

Production Secretaries: NABET.

Desk Assistants: NABET or WGA.

News Writers/Writers: WGA or NABET.

Associate Producers: NABET or WGA.

Field Producers: NABET or individual contract through your agent.

Associate Directors: Directors Guild of America (DGA).

Directors: DGA.

News Directors: Nonunion.

Producers: Those who double as on-air talent may belong to the Screen Actors Guild–American Federation of Television and Radio Artists (SAG–AFTRA); others may be members of the DGA; many are not members of any union and have individual contracts negotiated by their agents.

Executive Producers: Nonunion.

FUTURE TRENDS

The future of television producing and directing goes hand in hand with that of programming. Predicting either is about as accurate as predicting the stock market. Nonetheless, we can hazard a few educated guesses about future trends affecting those professions.

Let's assume that the cost of producing television programming will continue to increase. Increasing costs puts more pressure on producers to get higher ratings (and therefore higher fees from advertisers). There are conflicting theories regarding how this financial pressure may affect television production. One theory says that in order to control costs and retain as much profit as possible, the networks may start to produce more of their potentially lucrative entertainment programming in-house. The other theory says that in order to control costs, the networks will focus on what they do best—sports and news programming—and increasingly go to outside independent production companies for prime-time entertainment programming, foregoing the financial risk of producing a new program.

Production jobs, of course, will go whichever way the production trend goes. Wherever producers and directors work, though, it is likely that they will work in a more cost-conscious environment than in the past. This cost consciousness may affect both the type of programming and the nature of the producer's job. Financial skills have recently become an important requirement for a producer's job. A network personnel manager said that he has seen many MBAs come in and work as the right arm to producers and use financial analysis as a way of getting into producing. "Shows are more interested in the money than the creativity of the show," he said. "Money talks nowadays. We have many news producers coming in with financial backgrounds."

One predicted production trend is an increase in made-for-television movies and miniseries brought about by the public's reaction to premium movie channels (HBO, Showtime, Cinemax, etc.), and videocassettes. By the time most successful movies reach a network for their broadcast premiere, they have been so widely exposed on cable and videocassette that they have lost much of their traditional power to attract audiences. As a result, networks may find themselves much better off airing made-for-TV movies and miniseries, most of which are produced by independent production companies.

Other programming (and hence, production) opportunities may open up as a result of the pay channels' own problems with keeping audiences satisfied: It's hard to come up with enough movies to justify monthly fees since many premium channels are producing their own special programming (e.g., HBO's *Not Necessarily the News* and *Fraggle Rock*). Additional new programming should provide exciting opportunities for producers and directors.

The growing home use of videocassettes means there will be new opportunities for producing (and directing) original videotapes designed exclusively for home use.

Finally there are music videos. The overwhelming quick and healthy success of MTV and other music channels, as well as network programming (NBC's *Friday Night Videos*) has created a voracious market for music videos. The sheer number of five- or six-minute videos needed by 24-hour-a-day channels is staggering. In addition, music video channels are becoming as essential a promotional vehicle as a single. What's more, music groups may begin to produce 30- or 40-minute videocassettes as routinely as they do the traditional LP record album.

A Talk With . . .

Reuven Frank
Executive Producer, NBC News

> *Reuven Frank, former president of NBC News and now an executive producer of documentaries, has worked for NBC for 35 years. A graduate of Columbia University's School of Journalism (1946), Frank began working for NBC television during the summer of 1950 as a newswriter.*

I think I was the thirteenth person hired for NBC television news. There were six directors and seven writers. That was the total. Weeks after I agreed to take the job, I asked how much they would pay me. The guy who hired me, one of the writers, said, "We pay $100 a week." I said "I'm getting $100 a week" [as night city editor of *The Newark Union News*]. That was a lie—I was getting $90. So he said, "We'll pay you $110." Then I said: "NBC is a very big news organization. How come you didn't get one of your radio news writers who's been in the news business for years?" He said, "The guys in radio won't come to television because they don't think it has a future." That's how a lot of us got our jobs: People from radio news wouldn't consider television.

I like working in television for two basic reasons. First, it's news. The essence of the attraction of news to people is—or used to be—that however hard you work and however difficult the conditions, at least one day isn't the same as the last day. You could die of many things in news, but boredom is not one of them.

Second, when I began, television was a new medium. In those days it was the frontier. No one knew how to do it; and if you made a mistake, nobody knew you had because nobody had done it before. Now it's very rigid and institutionalized. In the old days, everybody did everything for a program. Today, jobs don't lap over. The medium has lost all of its flexibility, which is why all television news programs look the same.

Does the television business take over your life? Any job that interests and challenges you takes over your personal life. In our society your work defines you more than any other aspect of your life, more than your family, more than your origins. You are what you do. To say that television takes over your personal life is ridiculous. No one is obligated to work in television. This isn't Russia where they assign you a job.

Advice

Being in television is only glamorous if you think it is. To do it well is hard work, high skill, and some adventure. Only one person in a thousand is going to make a lot of money. The other 999 are going to be able to pay their rent. It is only the exception that is written about. Too many people on the outside judge television by the externals, by the press releases or stories in print and on television itself.

The essence of journalism is curiosity. Any journalist I would hire would have to have more than specific experience and the ability to report for the television medium. As a journalist you have to know history, science, and how a computer works, what the frontiers of biomedical research are. You also have to have some experience and familiarity with the economic forces in our society, why people lose jobs, what causes trade gaps, what creates work. The economy is something everybody talks about and nobody understands. The economy is what provides food and shelter for 250 million Americans. That's not an abstraction. That's a reality.

Generally the way to start is at a smaller station. With the buyer's market that now exists in television news employment, the networks can afford to insist on a certain level of experience and achievement. The smaller stations that don't pay as well are better for experience and to establish your skills.

I always advise people to try and find work in a city with between a quarter of a million and half a million population, where occasionally you'll meet people from the networks. If you start off in a little town of twenty-five thousand, you'll spend your whole career there. Not that that's bad if that's what you want. But if you're hoping one day to get a job in one of the networks or in a major syndicated operation, you have to have contact with the people there. If they never see you, they won't know that you're there.

A Talk With . . .

Hal Cooper
Director, Gimme a Break

> *Currently the executive producer/director of* Gimme a
> Break, *Hal Cooper's other directing credits include:*
> Search for Tomorrow, *80 episodes of* I Dream of Jeannie
> *and three years each of* Mayberry, RFD; That Girl; *and*
> The Odd Couple. *He was also director of* The Mary Tyler
> Moore Show, All in the Family, *and various episodes of*
> The Courtship of Eddie's Father, Hazel, Gidget, *and pro-*
> *ducer/director of* Maude. *Cooper got his start in television*

in 1948 at the age of 23, at (as he puts it) "the top of the bottom" as writer/producer/director for Dumont Television in 1948, the smallest of the three networks in the then-fledgling television business.

A guy I had worked for as a kid actor in radio said Dumont was looking for someone to produce some daytime programming for them. At that time there was no daytime programming, but Dumont was in the business of making television sets, so they wanted to have more programming to offer. I presented some ideas to Dumont, and they bought two of them. On November 1, 1948, the first day of all-day programming in television, I had two shows on the air—*Your School Reporter,* a news show for teenagers and *TV Babysitter,* a weekday morning show meant to entertain preschool children while mother was making the beds and the older kids went off to school.

The two shows were a huge success. *TV Babysitter,* which starred my wife, who was an actress and good storyteller, was such a hit that when we renegotiated our contract, our agent got us $150 a week instead of the original $75 we were paid. That fee was for the entire package of five shows a week and paid for my wife who starred in it, myself who wrote, produced and directed it, and all the props!

Now I'm mostly directing, though I produce also. As a director, I take all the elements of the production and try to get them to function at their best. I've got to be a psychiatrist, a mentor, a policeman, getting the performance out of the actors, consulting with the writer to rewrite or hone a particular section, trying to realize the essence of the show.

As a producer I see my role as protecting the director from the meddling of the producer . . . that may sound self-serving; but one of the reasons people try to produce their own projects, whether they are writers or directors, is that they want to protect their concept of the project at hand.

The theatrical aspect of television is the most rewarding part for me. In fact, one of the reasons I enjoy the sit-coms that I do is that, just as in theater, you perform in front of a studio audience that gives you instant feedback. In film and dramatic television, you don't have that luxury. You don't know what the audience thinks until maybe a year after you've finished it. What's fun about sit-coms is that if you do make a mistake, your studio audience will let you know and it's still repairable.

What do I dislike about the business? Nothing really. If I really didn't like it, I wouldn't be doing it. There are two things I like least, though. One is having to do things that the networks decide will be the most popular. Whenever you are serving the "God of the Most Popular," there's always a self-censorship process that goes on that either keeps the project from getting done or affects it in negative ways so that what you're doing could have been better.

The second thing I like least about television is the fact that there are only three shops in town where you can sell your wares: ABC, CBS, and NBC. We have other options now, such as cable, but there are still only three main stores. If you're not successful there, there's no place else to go."

Advice

Do I have advice for people? When I'm asked that kind of question I tend to try to discourage people from getting into the business. My approach is based on the theory that if you are discourageable, you shouldn't be in the business. If after you've been discouraged you still want to work in television, you've got a chance. The odds against success are tremendous. You just have to keep trying.

If you're interested in directing, there's nothing that exists in the world that can't be helpful to you. The more you know about lighting, the more you know about music, the better off you'll be. If you've acted, you'll know the problems of the actor; if you've written you'll know the problems of the writer. The more aspects of television production you have participated in, the more able you'll be as a director to get what you want in a production.

A Talk With . . .

Merrill Grant
Chairman and Chief Executive Officer, The Reeves Entertainment Group; Executive Producer Kate & Allie

> *Reeves Entertainment Group, a division of Reeves Communications Corporation, is responsible for the company's*

*television entertainment activities. Reeves Entertainment
is a producer of prime time television series, made-for-
television movies, game shows, and other programming
for network, cable, and syndication. In addition to his
post as chairman and CEO, Merrill Grant is executive
producer of* Kate & Allie, *the CBS hit situation comedy,
and was the creator and co-executive producer of* That's
Incredible, *the long-running one-hour series now in syndication.*

My route into television has not been the usual . . . I come
from the advertising agency business. I got an advertising degree from Columbia University's graduate school of business.
Then I went to Benton and Bowles and progressed through
their Media and Television Programming Departments. At a
point in time, it became apparent that the role of advertisers
had changed drastically. Their influence regarding which programs were actually scheduled on network TV had diminished
to such an extent that, if I wanted to be part of that creative
function, I had to leave the agency business. So I did.

The job I took was with Viacom which was then in the process of forming a production entity. I was hired in New York
to develop and sell programming to the networks. Thus I had
to get into the middle ground between production, which is
what I do now, and the advertising/marketing community
I was in then. I gradually progressed from there.

I have always enjoyed the development process more than
the production process; however, I think that most creative
contributions I make are generated in the area of development, i.e., working with writers in the stage preceding actual
production.

When projects we control are in production, I find myself
functioning more as a creative cop than as a filmmaker. When
concept, direction, and attitude have been agreed upon, it
becomes more important to make sure that all creative concepts are adhered to.

I like what I do because it is not *all* that I do. Television is a
small part of my life. I have a family, other creative interests
and my work. I intentionally live in New York where it is
possible to keep "the Business" in perspective. I am very anx-
ious to avoid the intrusive nature of the television business.
The monetary stakes are so high and the involvement is so

great that there is a constant threat of your job taking over your life.

Advice

I think one must understand that there is no mystique to the business of television—it consists of the fairly simplistic combination of creativity and good business practices. With a little bit of luck, some talent and a lot of honor, you'll do well.

A Talk With . . .

Francine Achbar
Executive Producer, WBZ-TV, Boston

As executive producer at WBZ-TV, the NBC affiliate in Boston, Francine Achbar is responsible for the station's productions of local documentaries, informational pro- gramming and public affairs specials. Her previous posi- tions at WBZ include executive producer of news and producer of specials, documentaries, and a weekly public affairs program. Achbar began her career as a newspaper reporter and competed for her first job in television as an associate producer for a talk show at WBZ by watching the program, offering a critique and ideas for program topics.

I got the job [as associate producer of a talk show] by "tap- dancing" harder than the other applicants. They asked for ten ideas for topics, I gave them 100. In addition to my 100 sparkling ideas, the woman who hired me said they chose me partly because they knew that as a reporter I knew how to write, research, and interview. "But mostly," she said, "it was my common sense." I had critiqued a segment of the show in which the host of the show was literally learning how to tap- dance but was wearing bell bottom pants. I said I thought it was pretty dumb of her to wear bell bottoms because you couldn't see her feet when she danced.

After a year and a half at the talk show, I got tired of recipes and interviews with former stars. So I went to a competing station in Boston as a newswriter and got promoted to show producer to assignment editor to specials producer to senior producer . . .

As an executive producer I now oversee the work of other producers. I'm not the player any more. I'm the coach. I discuss the concept, stay in close contact with the producers, and read all the scripts. Basically, I guide the project, hire, and motivate the people who produce.

I don't miss hands-on producing, really. I don't miss getting on the phone and doing research. I don't miss sitting in the back of the van and going on the road. I don't miss freezing in the rain while the talent tries to get the words right. Sometimes, though, I miss all the interesting people I used to meet doing the shows. I miss that direct contact.

What I like about executive producing is the parental role I play. I like watching producers succeed and watch them go on stage and win the awards. I also know how intense producing can be and how difficult, as a producer, it can be to see the forest for the trees. As executive producer, I can help the producer by giving them a clearer perspective on the show.

Advice

Go to the boonies, go wherever you can get an opportunity. Do whatever you're assigned to do. Don't think that you're going to walk into a Boston, New York, or Chicago and get a first job that's anything but entry level. Internships are very useful and can lead to freelancing and maybe permanent work.

It's a difficult and exhausting business. Remember that unlike a few big stars, most people in television don't make a lot of money. They do it for the psychic rewards. Most of the people who work for me are artists. They'll stay until three in the morning to make sure every edit is perfect. So, sometimes it helps to look at yourself as a subsidized artist rather than an underpaid producer.

A Talk With . . .

Missie Rennie
Senior Broadcast Producer, CBS Morning News

> *Missie Rennie's first television job was as a secretary/research assistant to the assistant bureau chief of ABC*

*News in Washington. She managed to get that job pri-
marily because she had political experience: She had
been assistant to John V. Lindsay's campaign manager in
the 1969 mayoral campaign in New York and had been a
staff caseworker for Senator Charles Percy of Illinois.*

I never really wanted to be in television. I always wanted to be
in politics. I took my first job at ABC mostly because I would
be working for the political correspondent. While I was at ABC
I heard about a new public television program that was going
to cover the political year. The show, produced by NPACT,
National Public Affairs Center for Television, was hosted by
Robin MacNeil and Sandy Vanocur and later Jim Lehrer.

I called NPACT and applied for a job as a researcher. They
said they already had researchers but had a production assistant job open. In the pecking order, production assistant is a
little lower than a researcher, and I wasn't sure if I should take
the job. So, I called a friend at ABC in New York who said: "A
researcher is a researcher is a researcher. But a production
assistant is an associate producer is a producer." I took the job
and six months later I was an associate producer and a year-
and-a-half later I was a producer/reporter doing on-air work
on my own pieces.

As senior broadcast producer for the *CBS Morning News* I'm
in charge of the line-up of the show each day. I take charge of
what stories to air, in what order, and for how long. It's constant work. The telephone could ring at three o'clock in the
morning because the lead guest has decided not to do a live
interview the next day. Or there is a major news development
overseas, and we have to throw out much of the line-up and
plan a new one in the few hours left before air. When you
work on a live news show that goes on at seven in the morning, you have to work 24 hours a day.

Why do I like what I do? It's like still being in school. Every day
you walk in and you learn something about a new subject. It's
extremely stimulating; you're always involved with new issues
and personalities. And there's an adrenalin that comes with
putting on a live show. The only atmosphere that seems similar is the trading floor of the stock exchange. The only problem is that it is a life that can be totally consuming. I try very
hard to make my personal and family life a priority, too.

Advice

Television news is a risk-taking business. Once you get your foot in the door, you need to constantly take risks. There isn't a single path; you have to create your own opportunities.

People can start at the networks as desk assistants or clerks and move up, but they should also be smart enough to know when to get out and have other experience. Local television remains an important training ground. I've also noticed an occasional curiosity—people coming into broadcast news from very different backgrounds. I know an editor in a publishing house who was hired for the documentary unit here because they felt he had good skills to determine what makes a good story.

A Talk With . . .

Gary Brasher
Producer, Director, Editor of PM Magazine, *Baltimore Orioles' Baseball, and News Programs*

> *While Gary Brasher's current television position is as chief CMX (a brand of sophisticated editing equipment) editor for California Video Center, editing such shows as* Falcon Crest *and* The All New Let's Make A Deal, *he has also been a television news director, sports director, and magazine show producer. (An interview with Brasher also appears on page 199 where he tells how he "snuck into television" as a studio camera operator in Houston.) What follows are some anecdotes from his previous lives as director of Baltimore Orioles baseball game coverage and producer of* PM Magazine *for a Columbus, Ohio station.*

After being a switcher in Houston, I moved to Beaumont, Texas, a much smaller market, because I wanted to become a director. It was really impossible for me to move up to directing in a large market like Houston; I could have stayed there for the rest of my life as a switcher. In Houston directors were hired because they'd been directors in a smaller city. In a small town like Beaumont, I qualified for directing because I'd been a switcher.

In Beaumont I directed local commercials, newscasts, public affairs shows, and elections. Then I moved up to operations manager—the guy in charge of all the cameramen, directors, tors, scheduling, and equipment. Then I was hired as a director exclusively for the news department of the NBC affiliate in Wichita, Kansas—a much larger market.

In terms of directing, being a newscast director is kind of an elite job because it's done live, and you have to think on your feet. If things go wrong you have to roll with the punches and recover quickly from mistakes. There's a lot of pressure in directing live newscasts.

Two years later I answered an ad in *Broadcasting* magazine—that's the place where you find jobs in local markets. The job was for news director for a tenth market station—KDKA, a Group W-owned station in Pittsburgh. I didn't think I'd get it and was honestly in shock when they called me for an interview . . . While I didn't get that job, they recommended me to someone at Group W's Baltimore station.

In Baltimore I was hired to direct Baltimore Orioles' baseball games. I had no experience in baseball, so I had to take a crash course in how to direct baseball, which is one of the hardest sports to direct. In almost any sport you can name—except baseball—as long as you follow the ball you've got the game. But in baseball, if you follow the ball, you miss half of the action. The pitcher may be holding onto the ball, but the guy on first may be stealing second base. The ball may be hit into outfield, but there are guys running around bases.

This was also about the time that Group W was starting up *Evening Magazine* [also known as *PM Magazine* in some markets], and I became director and associate program producer. It was a really exciting time because no one knew how to do this kind of show, and we created a system . . . About three years later, I left Baltimore and went to Columbus, Ohio's WCMH TV to produce *PM Magazine* for them.

The show had been on the air for about a year but was doing incredibly badly. . . . So, I went out and did shows in visible places like shopping centers so people would see us and go watch the show. Another trick I did was to cover stories about people who had a following—morning disc jockeys, important ministers. I figured if we only got a percentage of their followers to watch the show, we'd do well. And then I'd do provocative stories like an interview with a 40-year-old centerfold with as much nudity as I could sneak in. I figured that the next day at work people would talk about it. Fortunately for me and the station, it worked. The first rating book that came out after I'd been there (about two or three months after I started) we'd moved from third place to first place. It was the biggest shock I could ever have imagined.

<hr>

A Talk With . . .

Tom Weinberg
Producer, WTTW Public Television, Chicago

<hr>

> *Tom Weinberg is an independent producer and staff producer of* Image Union; *WTTW's program showcasing independent video. He is also chairman of the board for the Center for New Television, a Chicago media center and funding agency, a subsidized editing facility, and a teaching and training place for independent video.*

I have been producing shows off and on for WTTW for 14 years. For about half of that time I was a freelance producer, selling them pieces and shows. The rest of the time I've been on the staff there because we were producing *Image Union* and since I was representing the station, selecting the shows, and signing contracts, I had to be an employee.

I took some television courses in college [University of Michigan]. I got an MBA at New York University, and I suspect that some of the organizing I've been able to do came from that training—I never wanted the degree to climb a corporate ladder. I then went to work for $75 a week as an assistant something-or-other for WCIU-Channel 26, a UHF station in Chicago. I was hired originally to do the business and stock-market news because it was something I knew something about—at least they thought I did. That led to my producing, in 1969, *A Black's View of the News*, the country's first all black news show (I was, of course, the white producer). The guy who did the sports was Don Cornelius.

I eventually got into a fight with management and went into independent production. In 1972, Portapaks [portable cameras that were the forerunners of minicams] had just come out, and a group of 30 people with portable cameras and decks banded together. We called ourselves "TVTV" [Top Value Television]. We went to the Democratic and Republican conventions in Miami in 1972, and we shot and edited and did interviews. The equipment was black and white and fresh off the boat from Sony. Being on TV was a new phenomenon . . . people had never before really had cameras right up in their faces before. The stuff was very realistic. It aired on Manhattan Cable Television and Teleprompter [now Group W Cable]. Then Joel Chaseman of Group W saw it and decided to put this black and white stuff on all five of their TV stations.

Advice

My recommendation to people starting out is that you've got to expose yourself to as many different kinds of production, disciplines, and thinking as you can. Some of that means sacrifice—sometimes it's money, but mostly it's time and freedom. Sometimes it's pride and principle about what you would or wouldn't do . . . Remember, most productions are short. You can swallow a lot to learn a lot in a relatively short stretch of time.

A Talk With . . .

Cheryl Gould
Senior Producer, NBC Nightly News with Tom Brokaw

> *As the number two person reporting directly to the show's executive producer, Cheryl Gould oversees the writing, production, and line-up of stories on the network news program. She is also the producer in the control room while the show is broadcast, responsible for the overall program, including any editorial changes required while on air. Gould began working for NBC News in the Fall of 1977 in the Paris Bureau. In 1981 she joined NBC News in New York as a writer and within the next four years held eleven different jobs for the network,*

*including field, foreign, and domestic producing. Gould
was one of the creators and senior producer of* NBC
News Overnight *with Linda Ellerbee and Bill Schechner.*

I had no idea I wanted to be in TV. For the longest time I
wanted to be a pediatrician. Then I thought I wanted to be a
history professor. When I graduated from Princeton with a BA
in European history, I had no idea what to do for a living. I
thought: I know how to think, I know how to write, I know
how to ask questions, I've always been curious about world
affairs. So, I thought that might qualify me for a career in
journalism.

My first job in news was part-time as "Super Jock" for an ABC
affiliate radio station in Rochester, New York. Eventually, I
became a full-time radio reporter, cutting tape and doing
interviews. That's how I learned the ropes: how to make contacts with city officials, county legislators, the district attor-
ney's office, understand what people's concerns were in their
community. I also got to know other reporters for radio, TV,
and newspapers. And when a job became available at the
local ABC affiliate TV station, enough reporters knew me
and recommended me for the job of general assignment TV
reporter.

I like producing news very much. That doesn't prevent me
from complaining from time to time. It's very hectic; I have
very little time to myself—I work eleven to twelve hours a
day. But the work is interesting and carries with it a lot of
responsibility.

While what we're doing is not brain surgery, it is nonetheless
very important. We're trying to tell people what's happening
in the world around them, and at the same time to give them
assistance in making sense of it all. Some days are more fun
than others. When there is not much news going on, we have
to scratch our heads and figure out what we're going to say
after "good evening." Then, sometimes the news is happening so fast that it's changing while we're on the air. The adrenalin becomes its own reward.

For those of us who need instant gratification, this is the perfect
job. At the end of every work day you have a product that you
have put together. You don't have to wait until the next day,
month, or year to see the fruits of your labor. Sometimes it

turns out to be rotten fruit, but you're already working on the next day's news. As they say in this business, you're only as good as your last story.

Advice

The best advice I can give to people who are interested in going into the journalistic side of this business as reporters, writers, field producers is: Get a liberal arts education. You can certainly learn on the job how to use a tape recorder, what is a cutaway, and what is a wide shot. It's important to study history, philosophy, culture, and literature and to develop your critical capacities as a thinker.

In general, I recommend that you start in a small town first . . . I do know people who have started out as desk assistants at networks and have made it. But it takes a lot longer that way. When you're young, it's great to be out there doing your own field work, learning how to develop your skills and—just as important—developing the self confidence that comes from having to do it all yourself.

For more information about producers and directors, see interviews with Electa Brown (page 76), Brad Hagen (page 74) and Judy Seabridge (page 81).

5

WRITERS

Even though a picture may be worth a thousand words, the very visual medium of television needs writers for virtually all types of programming. In fact, in television, a world notorious for demanding rewrites from even the best, the writer's role is a vital one. So, while television writing may offer less autonomy than comparable work for the printed page, it does offer writers the potential for a rewarding, fun, and challenging career.

Television writing is different from writing for print. Like speechwriting or playwriting, it is meant to be spoken. In television, pride of authorship is impractical. Writing a novel involves two people—the author and the editor. In television writing, the editor, the producer, the director, and the performers may all have a hand in the script.

There are few full-time television writing jobs, and those that exist are hard to get. The good news is that if you are lucky enough to land a job writing for a show you love, the experience can be exhilarating. As a television writer, you are communicating with millions of people every week and can have the thrill of watching someone famous—or even not-so-famous—reading your words, hearing a studio audience laugh at your jokes, writing the script for an historic news broadcast, or overhearing someone on a bus discussing *your* soap opera.

The writer who hates the loneliness of most writing will be glad to learn that most television writing is a team effort. Most dramatic series have a group of writers working on the show;

news writers write in the newsroom; and soap operas have what they call "stables" of writers.

ESSENTIALS FOR THE JOB

You should know what makes a good story (whether it's news or entertainment), know how to tell that story, have an ear for humor, an understanding of drama, an understanding of people. You must also be able to write clear, well-organized prose and dialogue and know the language and its grammar.

As a news or entertainment writer, you should be able to work under severe deadline pressure. Whatever kind of television work one is in, whether network news, local programming, corporate/industrial television or entertainment, there are severe deadlines. You must also have an ego strong enough both to fight rewrites you disagree with and to put up with rewrites that you can't fight.

To succeed in television writing, you need persistence. If you are a freelance writer, as most television writers are, you can't let that persistence flag if you want to keep the assignments coming.

Versatility is a key to survival as a writer. That doesn't mean that specialization is bad; in fact, specialization is useful. Writers with a business or a science expertise have an edge over their competitors who don't if a program is in their area of expertise. But, in television, as in any mass medium, your specialty must be grafted on a broad general knowledge.

WHAT IS TELEVISION WRITING?

Writing for television means writing for both the ear and the eye: writing words that will be spoken and words that will go with pictures. You have to know what sounds right, not just what "reads." What's more, writing that is designed to accompany images requires special skill and practice. And finally, you have to write in terms of time—sometimes very short periods of it—and that presents a special challenge.

There are many kinds of writers in television. Television *news writers* write much of what the anchors and some reporters say on camera. *Entertainment writers*—especially those who write for situation comedies that are taped before live studio audiences—are essentially playwrights who have to write not just one play, but many little plays of a specific length: half an hour to an hour in length, minus commercial time.

Dramatic series writers are similar to movie screen writers. The biggest difference is that rather than write one movie, they write many mini-movies with the same core cast, week after week.

TV movie writers are screen writers, the only difference being the size of the screen for which they are writing. In television, telling the story is the responsibility of more than just the writers. There are a number of hybrid jobs such as writer/researcher, writer/producer, writer/reporter, writer/director, writer/anchor, writer/host, and writer/tape editors.

As a television writer you can work either in a full-time permanent position or as a freelancer. In most cases, both full-time and freelance opportunities exist for all types of programming. However, expect freelance writing positions for one-time programs such as miniseries, certain specials, and documentaries. Expect fewer full-time writing opportunities in corporate/industrial television where budgets do not always warrant having a full-time writer.

Despite the fact that television is a visual medium, writing is essential to a program's success, and good producers and directors know it. If the writing isn't good, there is a limit to what an actor, anchor, tape editor, producer, or director can do to improve on it. This is true of entertainment and dramatic programs as well as news and other factual programming.

Robin Leach, host of *Lifestyles of the Rich and Famous*, pays tribute to the writing of his show in an interview published in *Manhattan, Inc.* magazine in January 1986:

> The reason the show works and the reason people don't get jealous and don't become envious or all the other commandments—thou shalt not have avarice, thou shalt not covet, and thou shalt not whatever—is because there is a little tongue-in-cheek humor in the writing . . .

The reason for the frantic screaming voice, which has been described as halfway between the adenoids and the Atlantic, is because, just as the picture changes every three seconds, I want double the amount of copy in there to cover it. That was a conscious decision to wall-to-wall it with copy—instead of the normal 30 words a minute I try to get 60 words a minute. That's how we decided to write it, to help drive the pictures.

Some television writers say that if you want to write for television, you have to leave your ego at the door. What they mean is that often your writing is designed not to be noticed by viewers.

The seemingly casual patter in *Good Morning America* may or may not be ad libbing. Often it's been written by a writer and is being read by the host, off a teleprompter. The bad puns and slap happy jokes uttered by the game show host who is getting all the laughs (canned or not, they are still laughs), were probably written by a writer—not the host.

The searing questions posed by a network anchor to an important politician may well have been written by a news writer. In fact, the entire candid live interview may have been written in advance. A writer conducted a pre-show interview over the phone, edited it down to six cogent questions and answers, and reviewed them with the interviewee and the on-air interviewer. The result? A seemingly candid interview that succinctly covers the main points of a topic all within the three minutes allotted to that segment of the news program. But again, if it's done right, it doesn't sound written.

The writer of dramatic and comedic entertainment programs is actually a playwright and as such is responsible not only for the plot and the words, but for the parts of a story that are action with no dialogue.

Specific Formats and Lingo

Just as poetry offers the sonnet and other forms, television writing has its own distinct formats and lingo. For information about script formats, we recommend you read *Professional*

Writers Teleplay/Screenplay Format Book by Jerome Cooper-smith, published by Writers Guild of America, East (see Appendix for address). For information about script styles and lingo, we recommend *Television Production* by Alan Wurtzel (McGraw-Hill, 1983). You can also learn a lot by reading actual scripts. You can sometimes get copies of previously aired episodes of your favorite shows by writing to the producers.

A DAY WITH A TELEVISION WRITER ————

A writer's day depends a lot on the type of program you work for and the individual people working there, and, of course, whether you are freelancing or working fulltime for a station.

If you are working fulltime as a staff writer for a station, you'll find that the political climate differs from station to station and from department to department within a station. It even differs from shift to shift. As a freelancer for a station or a network, your work is similar to that of a full-time writer. The only difference is the uncertainty regarding how many and which days or nights you will work.

If you are a full-time entertainment writer, assigned to a series, expect a tough, grueling schedule during production time. The work week often stretches to seven days and the moment one script is in production, you have to start working on the next. You can also expect long hours, writing and rewriting.

As a full-time entertainment writer, you receive a hiatus between seasons, and you probably will need it. If you are a freelance entertainment writer, your day is like that of any freelance artist for almost any medium: a struggle with your self-discipline, hoping the phone will ring to interrupt you, and, on particularly bad days, phoning everyone you know to hear another human voice.

What follows are accounts of two actual days—one with a news writer and one with a station-produced entertainment show.

A Night With . . .

The News Writers at *The CBS Morning News*

> *On this morning network news program, which airs from 7 AM to 9 AM, there are four "newsblock" writers and one head writer. They are all responsible for the scripts of the news segments that appear five minutes after the hour and half hour. Depending on the head writer or copy-editor supervising the show, writers might be assigned to specific blocks and all the stories within their block, or to specific stories in each block.*

1 AM

News writers come into work. The first two or so hours are spent "reading in" which means reading the early editions of newspapers and the newswires for the previous several hours. There may be several scripts written by reporters earlier that night.

2:30 AM

The head writer begins assigning stories to the writers. The writers' task is not limited to editing reporters' scripts, but involves research and checking facts in the news library and by phone to bureaus, police officials, and other sources. The writers also work closely with a copyeditor, researchers, copy persons, the head writer, producers, and tape editors.

Often writers write scripts to accompany video tape that has already been cut by tape editors and producers. This sometimes is challenging because the pictures don't always tell the story, and the writer has to work around that.

3 AM

The head writer distributes a line-up of stories for the news-blocks. From this point on, the pressure starts to build. More and more stories have to be finished—videotape and scripts— and timed to fit exactly into the time allowed on the news-block schedule.

There is no break for lunch or whatever meal feels appropriate in the early morning. Grabbing a snack from a vending machine or a brown bag and eating at the desk is often the closest the news writer gets to taking a meal break.

6:30 AM

All stories have to be ready to go for the first newsblock. Meanwhile, other stories are being revised and rewritten as news development occurs. Even as the morning news show begins airing at 7 AM, writers continue to work on the upcoming newsblocks right through to the end of the program.

9 AM

The show is over. Writers leave the newsroom.

A Day With . . .

A Writer/Producer at *Good Morning America*

This is a sample day with a writer/producer specializing in non-news stories and segments. While the morning show also includes newsblocks, the majority of airtime is devoted to celebrity interviews and features about fashion, entertainment, sports, etc.

The day's schedule varies depending on whether or not the writer/producer's segments are going to be pre-taped with a guest or aired live. If the segment involves live airing, the writer/producer is likely to come in early that morning (5 or 6 AM) to help prepare the props and the guest. On days not involving live production and the long hours that sometimes go with it, the writer's day looks something like this:

10:30 AM

Writer/producer comes into the office. Checks up on stories in production and any new story assignments from the head writer.

11:30 AM

A story on gifted children is scheduled for the following week. The writer/producer talks to the booking department. Booking department members have located an expert on gifted children and several parents who might be good guests to have on the show. The writer/producer phones the expert guest and the parents and pre-interviews them. Each phone interview may take as long as an hour.

2 PM

Lunch.

3 PM

The writer/producer starts editing down the interviews to five minutes worth of questions and answers. "I pick out the key questions that I feel a mass audience wants to know," says a writer/producer. "For example, they want to know how they know their kids are smart, what they should do about it if they are. And I try to select the set of parents I think would be good to ask the expert guest questions."

5:30 PM

The writer/producer, who is responsible for any graphics or props that would be necessary to illustrate the story, goes to the videotape library to find some footage of children playing. Should the stock footage be inadequate, the writer/producer may arrange for a crew to videotape kids at a special school. Or perhaps the expert guest can be videotaped working with children.

6:30 PM

Writer/producer goes home.

CAREER PATHS FOR TELEVISION WRITERS

Career paths for television writers are as varied as the medium's programming. While there are writers who can write for almost any genre, this is not true of all writers. A person with a flair for situation comedy may not be able to write straight drama.

While there is no formula for becoming a writer nor for getting a television writing job, there are certain guidelines that may help. There are many paths to many types of writing; the process outlined here is a general, inclusive one. But when a job is exclusive to news or to entertainment, that will be noted.

There is no way to tell anyone how to write. Some people have a natural gift for it, others don't. And still others manage to acquire a workable skill though they may never be great writers.

For information about entry level jobs in television, see Chapter 2. For writers, secretarial jobs may be particularly useful first jobs, especially if you land one at a program you want to write for. In any of these entry-level jobs, be sure to perform well. Your enthusiasm, dedication, energy, commitment, and care even when it comes to typing and answering phones, show what kind of a person you are. If you do the little things well, people will be willing to give you a chance on bigger stuff—like writing.

Copy Person, Desk Assistant, Reader
See Chapter 4, pages 94–96.

Production Assistant
See Chapter 2, pages 33–35.

News Writer (News and Sports)
The title news writer covers a variety of writing jobs, mostly in larger market stations and networks. Smaller markets generally cannot afford the luxury of an employee who does only one thing.

News writers might write for news, special events, documentaries, sports, or other factual programming. They are expected to edit and write scripts for anchors, reporters, and correspondents, and edit and write all continuity (the patter that goes on between stories and leads into them). They get their information from wire services, photo service transmissions from still picture transmitting machines, newspapers, magazines, and telephone interviews.

Other responsibilities include matching videotaped or filmed news footage with appropriate sound bites and providing scripts that tie it all together within the allotted time limit—often as little as five seconds. To do so, the news writer spends as much time away from the typewriter as at it: working in editing suites, previewing videotape, working with producers and tape editors, and even supervising editing.

At the network news shows, full-time staff writers are generally assigned to the anchors and correspondents. They spend a lot of time with the anchors and correspondents to learn their style—what kind of phrasing they prefer, how they like to get into a story.

Your job is to produce scripts miraculously, exactly the way the anchor/correspondent wants to read them. Generally, most scripts are edited and sometimes rewritten by the talent. Staff writers come to understand that being rewritten by the anchor doesn't mean they failed: "Sometimes Charles Kuralt [CBS anchor and correspondent] would take a blank piece of paper and put it in the typewriter and my heart would drop," confesses a former CBS news writer. "But what was really important was not that he read on the air every word I wrote, but that the *ideas* I presented him were what got on the air."

It is rare to obtain a job as a television news writer if you have not had one before. The way to start is to get a job as a production assistant or desk assistant and work your way up into writing. The climb can be faster at a smaller station. Or you can get the required experience in radio or print journalism, even your school paper.

News writing opportunities also exist in corporate television. Good training for an aspiring news writer is to work on the company and industry news programs, which are sent out to their branches and plants nationwide. You'll probably also get hands-on production experience. Larger corporations with more sophisticated and professional departments have higher requirements.

Where to Apply

Send your resume, cover letter, and two or three of your best stories to the producer of individual programs at broadcast and cable networks and stations. For a corporate television job, contact the vice president or director of a corporation's television department.

Assignment Editor (News and Sports)

See Chapter 4, page 96.

Copy Editor (News and Sports) ───────────

Only large operations can afford a full-time copyeditor as a separate job not handled by a producer. Like their counterparts in print journalism, a copyeditor's responsibilities include reading all stories for accuracy, structure, and grammar.

To qualify for a copyediting job, you should have experience as a news or sports writer for print or television, or experience as a copyeditor for print, radio, or a smaller station.

Where to Apply

Send your resume, cover letter, and perhaps two or three writing/editing samples, to the producer of individual news and sports programs at stations and networks.

Continuity Writer (Entertainment) ───────────

A continuity writer writes the words that lead into and out of different segments of a program and into commercials. The familiar "We'll be back in a moment after these words from our sponsor" is an example of continuity writing. But so is the connective conversation for a magazine format show such as *20/20*.

Continuity writing is sometimes a separate job, but in a show like *PM Magazine*, it is part of the writer/producer's responsibility. Advertising and marketing copywriting for print and radio are good training, as is any kind of television writing.

Where to Apply

Send your resume and cover letter directly to program producers at game, talk, and magazine-format shows. Also contact agents who often have the inside scoop on freelance continuity assignments.

Promotional Writer ───────────

Promotional spots, called promos, are the ads you see on TV for upcoming shows. A promotional writer may be in a staff job in the station's marketing, promotion, or public relations department. Such a job is a good launching point for a show or news writing or producing job or for careers in advertising, marketing, and related areas.

Promotional writers may also be scriptwriters at an advertising agency. At smaller stations the promotional writers may actually be program producers or writers.

Writer/Producer or Senior Writer (Entertainment) ——

A writer/producer is either a senior writer in entertainment programming or a writer who also has producing responsibilities.

At *Good Morning America*, the non-news writers are called writer/producers, and their responsibilities include supervising the production, assembling props, tapings and edits of their segments. In addition, they are responsible for writing the scripts and generating many of the story ideas.

At a situation comedy or prime-time series, a writer/producer is a senior writer who supervises script writing on shows he or she has not personally written, or who is assigned more shows to write than others.

In corporate television, writer/producer jobs are most common since most corporate television departments are not large enough to warrant a staff member who only writes. The writer/producer handles each project from concept through final on-line tape edit.

Where to Apply

Most writer/producer jobs in prime time entertainment programming come through an agent. For station-produced shows (documentaries, news, talk, and magazine shows) write directly to the producer or executive producer of individual shows at network and cable stations.

Writer (Entertainment) ——————————————

The job of an entertainment writer is either a full-time contractual or a freelance position. Since you write scripts for the show, you must be thoroughly familiar with the show's main characters, the format and dramatic structure.

Where to Apply

Script assignments, whether long- or short-term are best procured through an agent. See page 142 for further information about writing for entertainment with and without an agent.

Soap Opera Script/Dialogue Writer (Entertainment)

For writers of soap opera, whether daytime television or a prime-time evening show, the logical first writing job is as a script/dialogue writer. Writers are usually initially hired for a six-script trial. Working from a story breakdown (an outline of the plot for that individual episode), provided by the head writer and breakdown writers (see next job descriptions), the dialogue writer writes a complete script for the assigned episodes. On soap operas most dialogue writers are assigned one episode per week.

Writing successfully for a soap opera requires total immersion in a show. It may take a dozen scripts before a writer begins to have the characters living in his or her mind. Unfortunately, some producers don't have the patience to give writers that long to develop.

Dialogue writing is grueling work, particularly for writers working for daytime television which has five episodes per week. "When a producer wants to sign a five-year contract with a daytime soap writer, I generally say 'no way,'" says agent Marie Stroud of Stroud Management. "After two years as a dialogue writer on one show, you begin to run out of things for the characters to say. You end up looking at the characters and telling them to shut up, which means it's time you moved on."

Where to Apply

Your best bet is to apply to agents (see page 142) or apply to writer development programs sponsored by Procter & Gamble Productions and CBS-TV. To find out more about Procter & Gamble's writer development program, contact the New York City office of Saatchi & Saatchi Compton, Procter & Gamble's advertising agency. For information about CBS's program, contact the writer development department at CBS-TV's entertainment division at its New York City headquarters.

You can also send unsolicited scripts to producers and head writers of shows you particularly like. While sending unsolicited manuscripts does not guarantee your material will be read, it sometimes works. Do not expect a reply right away—even if you have an agent. One agent estimates that it may take a year or two before a producer considers a new writer's work.

Soap Opera Breakdown Writer (Entertainment)

A breakdown writer works closely with the head writer to *break down* the season's story into individual plots for episodes called "breakdowns"; he or she is responsible for the direction of the show and how it leads up to its cliffhangers. Every episode of a weekly soap opera—not just the season finale—has a cliffhanger to get the audience to tune in the next week. In daytime soap operas, though, major cliffhangers occur every Friday to ensure that people tune in the next Monday. Part of the breakdown writer's job is to construct a plot that leads up to those suspenseful endings.

To become a breakdown writer, you should have experience as a dialogue writer. Writing breakdowns requires a special skill; not all good dialogue writers can do it.

Where to Apply

You need significant experience as a writer, which usually means you already have an agent. Your agent will contact producers for you. You may get promoted from dialogue writer to breakdown writer at a soap you are already working for.

Head Writer/Story Editor (Entertainment)

In episodic television, the head writer (sometimes also called the story editor) is responsible for the quality of all programs in a series produced during a season. This means overseeing the writers, the development of each episode, and sometimes writing individual episodes as well.

In soap opera writing, where there is one big continuing story, the head writer is responsible for the story over six months of programming. "Soap opera head writers have to be Scheherezade and Charles Dickens rolled into one, telling the neverending story," says soap opera agent Marie Stroud.

Head writers initially work alone to develop their story ideas. Later the producer joins them, and during the course of production, the breakdown writers and the dialogue writers as well. Some head writers also like to work on the breakdowns themselves to keep in touch with the program.

Another function of the head writer is to handle script revisions during production. The producer and director may have problems with a finished script. It may be too long, too short, or the actors may complain about certain areas. The head writer may personally handle the changes or supervise someone else.

Where to Apply

You will need significant experience as a writer. For entertainment, an agent must contact program producers for you. In news entertainment and magazine format shows, you apply to the program producer.

WRITING: THE PATH TO OTHER TELEVISION CAREERS

Writing is a natural path to producing, on camera reporting, hosting, and anchoring. Jane Pauley was principal news writer and reporter for the *NBC Nightly News* before she became co-host of *The Today Show*. Charlayne Hunter-Gault had been a reporter for *The New York Times* before becoming a correspondent for *The McNeil Lehrer Newshour*.

"If you surveyed the major producers and executive producers at the network news shows, you'd probably find a large percentage started as writers," notes a network news writer. "That's why threats of staff writer strikes don't have much clout—most of management knows how to write!"

Producing

As a producer, writing experience enables you to recognize good scripts and talented writers; it helps you to understand the structure and pacing of a story.

As a writer, on the other hand, you may find yourself attracted to producing because you would have more control over your story idea.

Reporting

Here you also should have writing experience; an on-air reporter should be more than just an actor on the scene of a news event. Many reporters, in fact, are writers or former writers, and some still write or edit their own scripts.

Hosting/Anchoring

Talk show hosts and news anchors are not always writers by training, though there are some whose writing gifts are much admired. Charles Kuralt of CBS is one. Edwin Newman, an NBC News correspondent and author of classic books on language is another. Some news anchors are also the show's managing editor and are responsible for the news content of the show, sometimes handling special reporting, researching, and writing. But even if the anchor/hosts can write, they usually do not have time and instead edit scripts prepared by writers.

Being a good writer and/or producer does not automatically prepare you for an on-screen career. Your writing skill has very little to do with being "telegenic"—looking and sounding good on camera and having that special charisma that attracts viewers.

HOW TO GET A JOB AS A TELEVISION WRITER

While Chapter 2 offers basic advice about how to get jobs, tips on interviews, resumes and reels, this section focuses on aspects unique to writing careers.

There are significant differences between getting a writing job in news and getting one in entertainment. Here, however, is some practical advice appropriate for all aspiring writers:

- *Know your subject.* Both news and entertainment writers should read newspapers and magazines. Current general knowledge is one of your best tools. Many television series and movies—not just news programs—tackle social issues. Being aware of what is going on in society and the world around you will help make your writing have more meaning for your audience.

- *Watch television.* One television writer made an early mistake in her career. She had good writing skills; she had good published samples; but, she watched very little television. This omission cost her dearly when the first questions at her first interview were: "What programs do you watch? What do you like and dislike about them?" You have to watch television, especially the programs for which you are applying to. If you think television offerings are lousy, analyze why you think they're lousy and how you would improve them.

- *Read newsletters.* If you are an entertainment television writer, or hope to be, subscribe to the monthly newsletters of the Writers Guild of America. There is an East and West edition. They offer news and feature articles, lists of television programs currently accepting script submissions, and notice of WGA seminars on writing for television and film. You don't have to be a member to subscribe. Write to one of the Guild offices for information about rates (see Appendix for the addresses).

  Books on programming and histories of television programming can also be useful. Check your local or college library for information.

- *Write, write, write.* The only way for you to find out if you can write is through writing. Write sample episodes of your favorite situation comedy or dramatic series. Many writers get interviews through sending out sample episodes to producers, head writers, and agents. It doesn't matter that the episode will probably never be produced; it only matters that producers have an opportunity to read it.

- *A writer's cover letter.* While we discussed cover letters in Chapter 2, writers should note that *their* cover letters are probably more important than those of people in other fields. Keeping it short, well-written, and to the point is critical. As the head writer at a network news show puts it: "When I get a cover letter I mostly look at the first paragraph of the letter to see if the person has been referred by someone I know or know of and then I look at the resume."

  While a letter does give some opportunity to show your writing ability—don't try too hard to impress. A baroque letter with too many attempts at humor or cleverness can backfire. What you think is cute may irritate your reader. The recipient of your letter is very busy. Be considerate. Get to your point quickly.

  Help the reader by laying out the letter clearly: "Use bullets or outline form in your letter," suggests a Los Angeles network television writer/producer. "Your points should jump off the page, because producers can't fight their way through a page of single-spaced prose."

  Entertainment writers should briefly state the subject matter of their script. Also identify its genre: half-hour comedy, hour dramatic episode, TV-movie, soap opera, etc. Don't succumb to the temptation to present what you have written as being adaptable to any format. It's confusing to the reader. Choose the most appropriate format for your story and state it.

- *Your resume.* Like your cover letter, your resume should be cleanly typed, well laid out, easy to read, and *short.* "I look for brevity," notes the network head writer. "I speak from experience. When I was out of college for just one year, I used a three-page resume to apply for a job working for a man I already knew. I was hired, but my boss later said that if he hadn't known me, he'd have thrown my three-page resume out. Now that I've been in the business for 28 years, I have a one-page resume. Anything more than one page is inflated. If you put too much detail, there's not much left for the interview."

GETTING INTO TELEVISION
NEWS WRITING

When you are applying for any kind of writing job, you need proof you can write. In news, you need the further proof that you can write on a tight deadline.

Many news organizations, especially the networks, use a writing test as a way of learning whether you can perform under pressure. Write to the news department, enclose your resume, and ask for an appointment. Be prepared to take a news writing test.

Preparing for the Writing Test

During the test, you will be given a roll of news wire copy and asked to write as many as ten news stories within a fixed period of time. Each story should be a specific length.

Before the test, you should practice writing to a specific time length so that you can quickly tell what a 20-second story is without having to waste time by reading the story aloud and watching the clock.

The test reviewer will be looking for clarity, accuracy, an appropriate selection of facts and mainpoints. Since wire stories present many more than you can use; the ability to capture the big picture without getting bogged down in detail is crucial as is the ability to do all this under deadline pressure.

A tip from the experienced: Before you take a news writing test, be sure to read all the news for the previous week. Pay particular attention to the newspaper published the morning of your test. Read it cover to cover! It is very likely that the test you take will be based on the wire copy of the day before.

Learning to Write

You know the old joke: A young man stops an old man on the street in Manhattan and asks "How do you get to Carnegie Hall?" The old man answers: "Practice, practice."

How do you learn to write? Practice, practice. Take any

opportunity you can get to write: your high school and/or college newspaper, radio or television station local community papers, local community-access cable television, and local radio stations.

Don't be discouraged if you have to start your writing career in a nontelevision format. There are many television reporters, writers, and other production personnel who have successfully made the transition from other media to television.

GETTING INTO TELEVISION ENTERTAINMENT WRITING

Unlike news writing, there is less of a defined career path for writers in television entertainment; there are no prescribed ways to break into the business. In order to succeed or, at least to begin, you need four things: persistence, luck, written scripts (produced or unproduced), and an agent.

Training and Education

Generally, you need exceptional talent for drama and a knowledge of television programming. There is no specific training that will help you as an entertainment writer. However, it helps if you have a four-year liberal arts degree from the best school you can attend. What you need more than anything is solid general knowledge rather than any kind of writing or communications degree.

A way you can get training and/or experience in television writing is by working in television production. Being an intern, secretary, gofer, or researcher for a show you like can give you an opportunity to observe the program in production, read the scripts, see the changes that occur, watch the actors and director work from the script.

Entertainment Writing Samples

In order to get work as a writer you have to have writing samples, published or unpublished. If you have no published samples, write some!

There are two ways you can begin: Write an original script for a proposed series or television movie or sample scripts for some show you enjoy. To work up a sample script, watch the show carefully. Immerse yourself in the program. Go to the library and look up articles about the show. See if there are books about the program. If the show is in syndicated re-runs, watch the re-runs. Get or borrow a videocassette recorder and tape the shows and study them. Watch them from a writer's point of view. Examine the dialogue, story structure, episode structure, and character development.

Only after you are thoroughly familiar with the show, should you begin to write your sample. A network program director suggests that you write to the program's producer and ask for a script for an aired episode. Better yet, ask for a copy of the script and its story breakdown, plus a story breakdown without the script. Study the script with its breakdown, then try to write a script to fit the second breakdown.

Your sample script or scripts really can get you an agent, or an interview at a studio. Writers have been known to use the same unproduced sample script over and over again to get interviews.

Other types of writing samples can also work well. One network vice president recommends that you attach a note to each writing sample explaining why you are submitting it. A short story may show how you handle dialogue; an excerpt from a novel may show character development or development of a story-line.

Some people say never send an unsolicited script; others say by all means do—what do you have to lose? Others have succeeded by writing to head writers. In the case of and producers, call in advance and ask what they prefer.

Make sure that the writing samples you submit look professional. They should be in the appropriate TV format, cleanly typed, double-spaced, and have your name and address clearly marked on the cover page. Also, attach a stamped and addressed envelope for your manuscript's return.

Getting an Agent

Once you have some writing samples you can start trying to get an agent. You need an agent because, in most cases, producers of prime time dramatic series, situation comedies, daytime soap operas, and game shows will only accept scripts submitted by an agent.

An agent is someone who represents you, who presumably has contacts at the major studios, independent production companies and networks and presents your work for you. An agent also negotiates your contracts and fees. In return, your agent collects a fee or commission, usually 10 percent of whatever you earn on the work he or she handles for you.

Unfortunately, it is difficult to get an agent. Most good agents have a full list of writers they represent; some won't even consider new talent. But there are agents who do scout for new talent. And there are ways you can try to get through to both the accessible and the presumably inaccessible:

- Through recommendations and referrals by friends and colleagues.
- Through directories. The Writers Guild of America, East and West, publish lists of agents you can send query letters to (see the Appendix for the address). The list tells you whether or not they accept unsolicited manuscripts. The Guild requires that you accompany all queries with a self-addressed, stamped envelope.

Proceeding without an Agent

Some producers do not require agent submission. Until you get an agent, focus on their programming. However, be aware that before a producer will look at an unsolicited script, you usually will have to sign a release form acknowledging that the producers may have already come up with your idea or one similar to it, and that you agree to specific limits on any damages for which you might sue should they produce something that resembles your script.

You can find out which programs need scripts by subscribing to the Writers Guild of America's monthly newsletter. A column called "TV Market List" provides the names, production company addresses and contact people for the shows that are not fully scripted for the season. The list also notes whether submissions have to be through an agent or if they can come directly from a writer. Unfortunately, almost all require submissions through agents.

Protecting your Work

As a writer sending out scripts, you should protect your original material from plagiarism or theft. A convenient way to do that is through the Writers Guild of America's registration service. Before submitting your script to a producer, send a copy to the Guild. The Guild will put your material on file, assign it a registration number, the date of submission, and send you a receipt. The WGA registration service is available to members and nonmembers at nominal rates.

The Interview

There are two kinds of interviews you can expect as an entertainment writer: with an agent or with the producer.

If an agent is interested in meeting you, based on your cover letter and resume, he or she may invite you in for an interview, possibly even before reading samples of your writing. Usually, the agent schedules the interview to get a sense of who you are. "I want to know how familiar you are with the programming," says a New York agent who represents soap opera writers. "I want to know which soaps you like, why you tune in. . . . Once I find that out, I want to see a sample of your writing."

Interviews with producers are similar, but if you have progressed as far as an interview with a producer (usually this happens through your agent), it generally is to discuss story ideas. If you are being interviewed by a Writers Guild of America signatory (a production company/studio that has an agreement with the Writers Guild of America to employ all writers under the terms of the negotiated contract), there is a limit to the number of times that you can be interviewed by the same company without getting paid.

UNIONS

In television writing there are several different kinds of unions and situations you might encounter.

In many small local stations, there is no union representing writers, copyeditors, assignment editors, desk assistants, and similar jobs. Work rules, salaries, vacation, etc., are up to the owners of the station, and they vary around the country.

In medium and larger markets, you are more likely to find stations under union jurisdiction. At these it is mandatory to join the union within a specific time after you begin work, usually within 30 days. The union, every few years, negotiates a collective bargaining agreement governing salaries, overtime, benefits, and work rules.

Most corporate television production and small independent production is nonunion. You negotiate your own salary and benefits.

In entertainment, full-time and freelance writers working for most major productions are represented by the Writers Guild of America (WGA). The Guild has relationships with both producers and writers. Producers and studios who agree to work with the Guild sign an agreement to employ all writers in accordance with the Guild contract. Such producers are called signatories. The Guild contract covers fees, payments, writing credits, and benefits for many aspects of television writing. The details are staggering.

You are eligible to join the Guild once you have sold your first television, radio, or screenplay to a Guild signatory or have a contract to write. As a nonmember, you can work for a WGA signatory, but you must join the union within 30 days. Once you do so, Guild working rules allow you to write only for WGA signatories.

To join the WGA, you pay a one-time initiation fee, dues and a percentage of your gross earnings.

As a freelance WGA member-writer writing for many different production companies and studios, you benefit from the pension fund just as you would if you were employed by a single company. What's more, you qualify for life and health insurance as long as you earn a set minimum in a given time period. In 1986, the minimum was $11,000 a year; the minimum is expected to increase annually.

The other union that might represent you as a professional television writer is the National Association of Broadcast Employees and Technicians AFL-CIO (NABET).

FUTURE TRENDS

With cutbacks of staff members at CBS and ABC, many staff writers may feel nervous. And with the networks and stations more and more conscious of the bottom line two things may happen: (1) more programming may be produced outside, and (2) there may be a movement to more hybrid jobs such as writer/producers.

The good news for freelance writers is really a result of the bad news for staff writers. Work that reduced staffs can not handle often goes to freelancers. The move to more programming produced outside the stations means more freelance writing assignments at production companies and studios.

The good news for all kinds of writers is the proliferation of new markets for programming such as cable television networks, stations, and premium cable services which gobble up programming faster than it can be produced.

There is also a growing number of videocassette recorder (VCR) owners. VCR owners are buying a wide variety of original videocassettes including instructional programming.

Another growing market is private television. According to D/J Brush Associates, some 8,500 companies and other organizations will have spent more than $2.3 billion producing their own video in 1986. This figure is more than twice the amount spent in 1981, when only 3,000 organizations produced their own internal video programs. Accordingly, writers and producers should continue to find work feeding the growing needs of corporate television.

A Talk With . . .

Al Wasser
Writer, ABC-TV's Good Morning America

> *Al Wasser has been head writer and writer for* Good
> Morning America *since 1983. His background is primar-*
> *ily news writing, including local and network radio*
> *news, and writing and editing for TV news programs for*
> *both ABC and CBS.*

Good Morning America is the first place I've ever worked that is not strictly hard news. Here the news segments are actually produced by the ABC News Division. I'm responsible for the preparation of live interview segments on the program. That means making sure that David [Hartman] or Joan [Lunden] are prepared to ask questions that will make for a fruitful or interesting interview.

Ninety percent of the writing I've been doing [for *Good Morning America*] is the hard news interviewing. I've been a newsman all my life, so that's my basic area of expertise. I've done interviews with people like Anatoly Scharansky and George Schultz.

I love what I do. I get to learn something every day about a whole variety of things . . . There's a thrill of knowing things before everyone else does. That's what got me really hyped. I remember working on my college radio station in 1956 when I read over the wire that France and Israel had invaded the Suez Canal—I interrupted the music to tell the news . . . I regard news as a branch of education. Some of the proudest moments of my career were when I was working in local radio and I would use a two-line story in a newscast, written well enough so that someone would call up and want to get more information.

Advice

Ultimately, the most successful new entries into broadcast news are those people who know the English language and grammar, who know how to spell, who know how to choose the words that best convey the information . . . People with command of the English language seem to be in dwindling supply as new generations of students come out of our school system.

. . . If you have an ego about your writing, you may as well forget it. The purpose of a broadcast news writer is to make the anchor look and sound good on the air. I've written for Bob Shieffer, who used no adjectives and Charles Kuralt whose strength is his ability to use a greater vocabulary and be much more expressive. And you should also have a real interest in news, a real interest in what's happening in your community, your country, your world.

A Talk With . . .

Carmen Finestra
Writer/Producer, The Cosby Show

> The Cosby Show, *NBC's hit comedy series starring Bill Cosby, has seven staff writers including one head writer, two writer/producers (senior writers) and four writers. Carmen Finestra began on the show as a writer during its first season and was promoted to writer/producer at the beginning of its second. He has been writing for televi-sion since 1976, has been a staff writer for* Angie, *and has written for Johnny Cash specials, Steve Martin specials,* Chico and the Man, Good Times, *and* Love Boat.

I started in New York as an actor. I came to New York to be-come a stand-up comedian and got into acting because some-one was doing a production of *Tom Thumb* and was looking for a short actor. I'm five feet tall so a friend recommended me. The producer asked if I could act; my friend said, 'I don't know, but he's five feet tall.' I got the part.

Through the theater I made a contact with Joe Cates [who produced the original Broadway production of *Joe Egg* and country music television specials]. I took a job as an office boy for Joe during the day and acted at night.

Meanwhile I was always writing sketches, spoofs of plays I was in, crazy memos at work, etc. Then, in the summer of 1976, Joe Cates was going to do a four-show variety series with Johnny Cash in Nashville. I wrote a couple of sketches as an audition. He loved it and I was hired for those shows. That was where I met Steve Martin and later I wrote several spe-cials for him . . .

On the whole I enjoy [writing for *The Cosby Show*] a lot. I began in this business thinking I'd be in front of the cameras. But I find I enjoy being behind the camera very much. Instead of being one character, I get to be involved as a writer with several characters. I enjoy being able to express myself and see my ideas come right from my mind and go to a national audience . . .

Advice

You can get very low paying jobs for shows. Just to see how a show is run is very useful. You are around people who are doing the show and you can see they are no different from you. It eliminates the intimidation factor, so that you don't have to be in awe when you come in contact with these people. Seeing how a show is written also gives you a better idea of how to do a show. One important thing about being a writer is never being afraid to throw it out. If you think that what you've written is in stone, you'll be in big trouble in the television or film industry . . .

You have to keep writing. Write a sample script of a show you really like, submit it to agents, submit it to producers. The only way to get into television writing is to keep writing and make your writing available to people who can help you . . . I don't think any training leads up to it. You just have to sit down and write. You have to learn discipline. Study Latin—they say Latin is good for discipline, at least that's what they told me in school . . .

A Talk With . . .

Allan Leicht
Writer and Producer of Television and Movies

> *Allan Leicht is an Emmy Award-winning television writer whose credits include* Kate & Allie, Ryan's Hope *and the NBC-TV movie* Adam. *Before discovering that writing for television could be an honorable way to earn a living, Leicht directed plays for the Studio Arena Theater in Buffalo, New York. His last theatrical directing job was the off-broadway production of the American premiere of* The Brass Butterfly *by William Golding.*

I always thought of myself as a dramatist—someone who works in the theater. I was writing plays and in 1968 or 1969 I sent one to a distant relative of mine who happens to be Alan Landsburg [of Alan Landsburg Productions]. I didn't hear anything for about a year. Then he called and said "I read your play. How would you like to write a movie?" So I did. But it never got produced. And then I wrote another for him. But *it* never got produced. But I did get into the Writer's Guild and Alan's was at least one office I could get into. It was fitting that my first big success should have been *Adam* for Alan's company. Also, through Alan I met Merrill Grant [chairman of Reeves Entertainment and executive producer of *Kate & Allie*].

My first steady job as a TV writer was for a new soap opera called *Ryan's Hope*. I loved it. It was the first year of a new soap opera, so it wasn't too sudsy—the characters and plot hadn't become routine yet. The people were wonderful and I did some very good writing. In a way, you can write with more freedom for daytime shows than for prime-time—the audience is more tolerant during the day and very loyal . . .

After *Ryan's Hope* I went back to freelancing. I wrote a couple of features. They never got made. I wrote a couple of *Movies of the Week*. They never got made. I wrote at least a half a dozen pilots, none of which got made. And, I worked on lots of developmental projects. And none of them got made.

Then came *Adam* and it got made [NBC-TV, October 1984]. It was about an abducted child who was killed and it addressed the issue of missing children. That project took about two years. Did I enjoy it? It's hard to say that I enjoyed it. It was enormously demanding, emotionally. Was it a positive experience? Yes. That movie actually changed the world a bit. It changed how we see ourselves. It showed people that we as a society don't care very much about children. Almost never does a writer get a chance to do something that has an effect on the way so many people think and live. I'm enormously proud of *Adam*.

After *Adam*, I worked on *Kate & Allie* as a co-producer/writer. I wrote for them for the show's first year. A lot of the writing was by committee and it was fun because the people were fun. If people can leave their egos at the door and come in to get things done, the work can be very satisfying.

I like to write for television. I don't like everything I write, but I like the process of writing. It's a very respectable way to earn a living. You have a great deal of variety and you are part of the mainstream of American culture.

Advice

Write as much as possible. That's the key. A lot of it is luck. Also a lot of it is survival and sticking to it, finding ways to survive while you are doing what you want to do. You also really have to write well. That would seem to be obvious, but it takes a long time to learn to do that. It's hard work—even physically taxing. The most important thing is to have respect for the medium, for the audience, and respect for yourself. And have a high tolerance for disappointment.

A Talk With . . .

Judy Tygard
Writer, The CBS Morning News

> As a staff news writer for The CBS Morning News, Tygard is responsible for writing news stories for anchor Faith Daniels. In addition to writing, Tygard also copy-edits for the show when the regular editor is sick or on vacation.

My introduction to the television news business was as an intern at a local station in New York City. I walked into the news director's office that first day and there he was, standing by his desk wearing a pith helmet and cracking a bullwhip. It was his idea of a joke, but that was my first impression of a television news director and I wondered what kind of business I was getting myself into . . .

As an intern, I worked on the assignment desk in exchange for college credit. I answered phones and got coffee and also learned to monitor police and fire radios and to move crews. After I graduated, the station had an opening for a desk assistant on the assignment desk and I got the job. It was really a lucky break. Basically, they took me because I had done well as an intern. Besides, the pay was so low that not a lot of people could afford to take the job. As it was, I had to take odd jobs just to survive—typing at weird hours, working as a messenger . . .

My career there was not all linear. At first, I moved quickly from desk assistant to night assignment editor to weekend assignment editor. I moved on to become a news writer, copyeditor and weekend producer and within two and a half years, I was producing the ten o'clock news during the week. But inbetween I had some setbacks. Once I blew something on the desk and was demoted to a script production assistant. The only reason I stayed at the station was because my confidence was totally shaken. But I worked my way back . . .

A lot of my friends think what I do is glamorous. But when you're writing the Burmese typhoon story for the third time at three o'clock in the morning, you don't feel glamorous.

The pressure is high in television news—but it's not all negative. It's exciting to have an axe hanging over your head. But what fascinates me most is that the stories themselves change all the time and you get to know about events before anyone else does. When the news bulletins come in and you're scrambling for information, that's when the adrenalin starts to flow.

Advice

I studied broadcast journalism in college, but in retrospect I would not advise anyone to do that today. What you really need to be good in this business is to know as much as possible about everything. I learned too much about skills instead of getting a broader education. Since I graduated from school, I've had to study a lot on my own.

Working at a local station was a great way to begin. Smaller stations are willing to take risks with young people. They have limited resources and so it's a mutual attraction. They need you and you need them. So, you really get a chance to do a lot. I produced two documentaries at the local station and I went to Rome to cover the elevation of New York's archbishop. It gave me a very wide experience.

Expect to work crazy hours. It's not so bad—in fact, it can be refreshing. The problem is that your circle of friends gets very small and you always feel like you're eating breakfast.

A Talk With . . .

Marie Stroud
Soap Opera Writers' Agent

> *Marie Stroud, of Stroud Management, represents a dozen soap opera writers. In the past, she wrote scripts for* The Doctors.

It is certainly possible to break into soap opera writing. That's not to say it isn't a tight little group. Writers and producers do have a tendency to recommend and hire writers they know, but it's still possible to break in.

What you need is patience and determination and I think you need an agent. But even with an agent, it can take about two years to get the hirers to read your material and consider you. There is a valid reason for this long stretch. It's difficult to put together a package [a team of writers for a soap opera] that really jells. So, once they have a good team, producers are reluctant to change it. You don't just fire one writer because you want to try someone new.

I don't know how it works with other agents, but I do take phone calls. You can call me and set up an appointment. I like to talk to you before I read your work. I want to know how familiar you are with soaps, which soaps you like, why you tune in. I want to know what intrigues you about the medium. Then, if it makes sense, I'll want to see some of your work, something that shows the ability to write dialogue, your sense of character and conflict. It doesn't have to be a soap opera script. It could be a play, a short story, a section of a novel. What I want to see is characters inter-relating and in confrontation. Long descriptive passages and stream of consciousness just don't work in soap operas! If I'm impressed, I'll start trying to get your material to people in positions to hire writers.

If I'm lucky, a writer will get assigned a sample non-air script. The producers will send the writer a breakdown to write from. Typically, if that one works out, the producers assign the writer up to six on-air scripts as a trial. This is unfortunate. I think it takes at least thirteen weeks on air for a writer to home in on the flavor of the show and characters.

To write for soap opera, you should be able to close your eyes and hear the characters talking in your head. Their voices should be so distinctive that you know which one is talking. The characters have to be real to you. Ask anyone why they are addicted to a particular soap opera and they'll tell you it's because of the characters.

Advice

If you're just starting out, I think you're best off trying to get an agent. But, you can send your scripts to network writer development programs, producers or head writers. I got my chance through a head writer. My first script was for *Another World*. It included among other gross mistakes a one-page monologue for a character. The head writer was very kind. He called and said: "First, daytime drama is not about monologues. Second, even if it were, you picked an actor who can't remember more than two sentences at a time. Go back to the drawing board and watch and listen!"

The most important thing a young writer can do is to watch soap operas. So many people wake up one morning and say they want to write soap operas, but they have never really watched them. You have to watch and listen to the programs and analyze them from the point of view of the writer. But, most of all, you have to love soap operas.

Schools do teach soap opera writing, but I think the best teacher is first watching and writing yourself. And then, if you can train under a soap writer, that's the ticket. In my opinion, *Knots Landing* is the best school for soap opera writers—both aspiring and working. *Knots* is built on interaction of character. The plots come out of the characters themselves and are not superimposed on them. Watch *Knots Landing*—it's what daytime soap operas should be all about.

6

Television Engineers

You turn on your television set and see brilliantly colored fish gliding in and out of intricate coral reefs; you hear the bubbling of an underwater diver's oxygen tanks and the splash of salt spray. Jacques Cousteau is once again bringing the exotic ocean world into your living room . . . with the help of more than just his camera and audio crew.

Television is a visual and auditory medium. How good a picture looks and sounds on your television screen is not only a function of your television set, your reception, and the production quality of the program you are watching. It is also a function of the transmitting station's engineering capabilities. The quality of what you receive is directly dependent on the quality of what a station transmits.

Quality of the video and audio signals is the primary responsibility of television engineers. Television engineers are responsible for the error free functioning of a television station, production house, or department. This responsibility includes the design, purchase, documentation, installation, operation, maintenance, and repair of all equipment. It also extends to keeping the station or department updated on the latest developments in audio/video technologies and on technical regulations affecting the industry.

Television engineers are responsible for equipment that includes videotape editing equipment, studio cameras, film projectors, remote relay equipment, mobile telecasting units, special effects devices, videotape recorders, transmitters, antennae, and telecommunications devices.

The job opportunities in television engineering range from the entry-level post of technician to the position of director of engineering (sometimes called chief engineer). Between those two extremes is a diversified group of engineers who specialize in maintaining and operating equipment, designing audio/video systems, installing television systems, and more.

The outlook for television job opportunities is good for engineering graduates. In fact, some broadcasting companies actively recruit at college campuses and have difficulty finding enough quality electrical engineering graduates. They have difficulty because television is a 24-hour-a-day business with round-the-clock shifts. The lure of normal hours can be compelling.

Why would an engineer want to work in television? Basically, it's the love of show business. Being part of the team that makes television programs look and sound their best, being part of news production or the burgeoning business of television computer graphics can provide an exciting career.

THE SCOPE OF TELEVISION ENGINEERING ────

In television, engineering is a broad category. Among the professionals called engineers are audio/video design engineers (also known as broadcast systems engineers [BSE]), maintenance engineers, field engineers, operating engineers, and research and development engineers.

Department Structures ───────────────────────

The structure of engineering departments varies greatly. The size of an operation and the corporate structure affect the engineering department setup.

At NBC network headquarters in New York City, for example, the audio/video design engineers are members of the National Association of Broadcast Employees and Technicians (NABET), a union representing a large number of television employees. At ABC and CBS they are part of management. At CNN, the engineers and other technically-oriented personnel are not full-time employees of the network but independent contractors.

Generally, the larger the station the more segmented is the individual job of an engineer. At a smaller station, the job usually involves a broad range of responsibilities—from maintenance to operations to administration to work in the field. The drawbacks of work at a small station are that the range and sophistication of the equipment is less than at a network or large market station, and salaries are usually lower.

Television engineers in any television environment fall into one or many of the categories described next. At a network, the groups and their functions are likely to be more segmented and represent the full range of opportunities.

Audio/Video Design Engineers

Audio/video design engineers (also known as broadcast systems engineers) are responsible for designing, purchasing, and installing all broadcast systems, such as special effects production rooms, editing suites, videotape recorders, transmission and master control rooms, television studios, and mobile units for on-location (also called "remote" or "field") production.

In addition, at CBS and NBC there is a group of *special services* or *systems services engineers* who are responsible for small-scale, urgent, and quick turnaround projects.

Supporting the audio/video and special/systems services engineers are the *design drafting engineers* who draw the blue prints for systems and equipment to be installed; engineering/construction technicians—technicians, mechanics and wiring specialists responsible for wiring, assembling, building, and installing any type of broadcast equipment or system.

Maintenance Engineering

Maintenance engineers are responsible for maintaining and repairing all types of broadcasting equipment. The structure of a maintenance department varies from network to network and from station to station. In one network, the maintenance engineers may have maintenance responsibilities for equipment ranging from videotape recorders to computer graphics equipment. In this case, the department is centralized, and the network departments turn to one maintenance group for all their needs.

At another network, maintenance engineers specialize in specific types of equipment and/or locations; one maintenance group may be assigned to studios, another to post-production equipment, one to graphics, one to news, etc. This is a decentralized system.

In medium to smaller market television operations, the maintenance engineers, as most other personnel in smaller stations and environments, have a broader range of responsibilities than they would in a network. In these smaller shops, there is much more pressure on the individual engineer.

Field Engineering

Maintenance engineers often work outside a studio for on-location recording for news, sports and some entertainment programming. Field engineers may do a lot of traveling, depending on the programs they are assigned to. Foreign news assignments, such as the Reagan-Gorbachev summit in 1986, take a field engineer to Iceland. Sports events require a similar level of traveling.

The type of work and the pressure involved vary according to whether the program is airing live, or broadcast that day on a news program, or for an entertainment program with scenes shot out of the studio. Field engineers specializing in news and live coverage have the least predictable daily schedules.

In smaller markets, there are fewer total programs going on the air, but there are also fewer crew members for each program. Field engineers in smaller markets, therefore, may perform several jobs, including lighting and editing back at the station, in addition to their field engineering responsibilities.

Operations Engineering

Operations engineers or technicians operate the videotape recorders and associated hardware, such as audio/video test and communications devices. This group includes people who perform basic editing, inserting, and assembling different portions of videotape onto one tape. They may also act as assistant to videotape editors. In addition, the group includes those who operate graphic equipment to create titles and names, and the machines that play the commercials during a broadcast.

Many equipment operating positions are extremely high-pressure, especially those that involve live transmissions and news production. The pace is often hectic, and the pressures of live production or severe deadlines demand flawless and speedy performance.

Research and Development Engineering

At the three major networks that can afford the luxury of research, research and development engineers (R&D or technical development engineers) are responsible for ensuring that the network is at the leading edge of broadcast and communications technology, keeping its facilities as up to date as possible, and creating new methods for improving broadcast quality. They are concerned with the improvement of such audio/ video technologies as stereo audio, satellite transmission, new technological formats, and high definition television.

TELEVISION PRODUCTION EQUIPMENT

What follows is an excerpt from *Broadcast Management/Engineering*'s 1985 list of "TV/Teleproduction's Most Wanted Products" (February 1985). The list ranks television equipment according to amount purchased by stations and production studios in 1985. The information shows both the overall pattern of purchase in 1985 and the pattern within different markets.

The list is a useful guideline to the kind of equipment you may encounter as a television engineer. It also shows what recent equipment priorities were in particular market places. Accordingly, you may want to invest in a training course on repair, installation, or use of some of this equipment.

1985 Rankings: Television Production's Most Wanted Equipment

Equipment	Overall Ranking	Top Ten Markets	11–50 Markets	51+ Markets	Tele-production
ENG cameras	1	7	2	2	12
Character generators	2	2	12	1	10
Studio/field cameras	3	4	3	11	3
Digital effects devices	4	9	8	8	11
Video monitors	5	3	14	9	1
Studio cameras	6	15	1	18	19
Time base correctors	7	6	15	3	31
VTRs, one-inch	8	1	4	12	5
VTRs, 1/2-inch	9	5	11	19	14
Power supplies/ batteries	10	19	5	15	8
VTRs, 3/4-inch	11	8	19	6	2
Lighting and camera support	12	25	9	5	9
Production switchers	13	18	7	13	4
Audio consoles, equipment	14	17	6	21	18
Routing switchers	15	10	24	10	16
Test equipment	16	12	10	25	7
Frame synchronizers	17	21	32	7	21
Time code equipment	18	13	13	27	15
Satellite earth stations	19	30	30	4	N/A

Equipment manufacturers often offer such courses at reasonable prices. See the vendor-sponsored training courses listed in the Appendix.

CAREER PATHS FOR TELEVISION ENGINEERS

There are two basic routes for television engineers. One is for the person interested in operating equipment; the other is for the person interested in how the television system operates. What follows is an outline of ways to pursue these two career paths.

For production assistant, intern, and other entry-level jobs. At a small local station, apply for entry-level positions through the engineering department. Usually there is less competition than for a position on the production staff (as opposed to crew) and thus a better chance of a job where you can learn the technology that interests you. In addition, the engineering department is likely to appreciate you more than the "creative" production department, which usually seeks aspiring producers rather than engineers for interns and production assistants.

Operator Engineer Career Path

Videotape Librarian

The position of videotape librarian is semi entry-level at a network or large station. The librarian distributes tapes to staff members and keeps them in order. The videotape library is the storage area for all videotapes—past and present—produced by the station. Private television departments are not likely to be large enough to warrant a full-time librarian; library duties will probably be the responsibility of production assistants and interns.

As a tape librarian you should be prepared to work all hours. You can expect a hectic pace at times, especially in news divisions.

Where to Apply

Contact stations and ask for the name of the library manager. Also ask if there are several libraries since some networks and large stations have separate libraries for individual departments. Write to any and all of the library managers.

Videotape Operator

To be a videotape operator, you must have previous television experience as well as technical training and you must be able to do more than just turn on a videotape recorder. You are responsible for seeing that the recorder is recording at proper levels for both video and audio. You must be able to read signals on a waveform monitor and vectorscope.

Other responsibilities of the videotape operator include

duplicating (dubbing) tapes and checking them for video and audio quality. In addition you should learn enough about the equipment you are handling to be able to solve routine equipment trouble. If you are participating in a remote or field shoot, you may not have immediate access to maintenance personnel and must be able to make basic repairs.

In a network, your position may be rigidly defined. However, you may have opportunities for training as an editor, audio engineer, or other position. You may get some training on different videotape systems so you can substitute for other operators when they are sick or on vacation. Performing well as a vacation relief person can of course lead to a promotion.

At a small station, production house, or private television department, the title of videotape operator may not even exist. With the title of engineer, you may actually perform the tasks of a videotape operator, a camera assistant, an assistant editor (setting up tapes during an edit for an editor and/or operating a playback machine), or a character generator operator. You may also act as an editor, assembling videotape segments and even full programs.

Where to Apply

For a network position, contact the videotape operation manager or post-production manager. For a job in a small station, contact the director of individual programs. For example, contact the news director who can pass your resume along to the person who is in charge of hiring technical personnel. In the case of cable television, you should phone the station and find out if the technical personnel are hired directly by the station or are hired through a technical staffing organization, as they are at Cable News Network (CNN).

Videotape Editor and Post-Production Videotape Editor

See Chapter 7, pages 192–193.

Audio/Video Engineer Career Path ───────────

Engineering Technician/Construction Engineer ──

An engineering technician, also called a construction or implementation engineer, is responsible for wiring, building, assembling, and installing television systems or individual pieces of equipment. Technicians, even at the network level, work for almost all departments involved with technical production. They handle all kinds of equipment, including audio/video switchers, audio/video tape recorders, cameras, microphones, test equipment, lighting equipment, etc. for both on-air and off-air use.

This is an entry-level position that requires a basic grasp of the fundamentals of electromechanical engineering which you can get in a technical school or college. As with most engineering jobs, a technician will gain the richest experience from work at a smaller station or production house rather than at a network.

Where to Apply

For a network position as an engineering technician, find out the name of the person within the engineering department in charge of the technician group. Unfortunately, since the name of this technical group varies from station to station, you may have to do some phoning to find out the structure of the department at each station to which you apply. One network engineer recommends finding out the name of the supervisor who is a union member rather than the nonunion manager. The technicians' supervisor can be a good source of information about both permanent and temporary job openings.

A particularly good way to get your foot in the door when job openings are tight is through vacation relief—substituting for permanent personnel who are on vacation. These temporary positions are usually for several months and are often extended if you perform well. While there are no guarantees, they can lead to a permanent position. The union supervisor or a friendly department secretary may be able to tell you when vacation relief applications are accepted.

Maintenance Engineer

"A maintenance engineering position can either be looked at as a stepping stone to other engineering jobs, or as a career in itself," says a network engineer who got his start as a maintenance vacation relief. "If you enjoy the challenge of solving problems, fixing things and working with your hands, maintenance can be very rewarding. As a stepping stone, however, it is an excellent way to really learn the equipment used in television production."

Maintenance engineers are responsible for the upkeep of all the electronic equipment and systems for television production (switchers, special effects, videotape recorders, etc.). This involves repairing or arranging for the repair of broken equipment, and performing routine diagnostic checks to minimize the chances of equipment failure. In television, equipment failure can be expensive, especially during live transmission because valuable commercial air-time is lost. It is also expensive during a taping session during which entire crews and casts may be standing idle while critical equipment is being repaired.

Other maintenance engineering responsibilities include upgrading equipment and recommending new state-of-the-art equipment.

As a maintenance engineer you can work either in studios or in the field. A field maintenance engineer is assigned to a field unit (the crew that goes out of the studio to videotape events). Field maintenance offers the engineer the extra challenge of having to cope with new and unknown situations. Improvisation, creativity, and quick thinking are particularly useful for field work where anything and everything unexpected happens.

At the network level, engineers may be assigned to a specific type of equipment, such as videotape recorders, graphics equipment, post-production, etc. In some cases, maintenance engineers are expected to be proficient with all kinds of equipment.

In smaller stations, cable, production houses, and corporate television, there may be only the position of engineer, a catch-all title that describes a person who acts as both an operator and a maintenance person, in the studio and outdoors, during live transmissions and prerecording tapings.

Where to Apply

For a maintenance position at a large station, phone and ask if there are separate maintenance departments organized by type of equipment or if there is one centralized department. "If there are several maintenance departments, apply to the specific maintenance department that relates to your expertise," a network engineer advises. If the department is centralized, write to the manager or director of maintenance engineering.

If you are applying to a production house or a small station without a maintenance engineering department, apply for a job as an engineer and present your maintenance skills as your selling point.

Special/Systems Services Engineer

Almost exclusively a network position, a special services or systems services engineer (the name varies from place to place) is the television engineering equivalent of the Delta Force. It's a crackerjack team of engineers who work on urgent and quick turnaround projects. When there is no urgent project, they modify existing equipment and systems, evaluating them to determine whether they need changes.

Special services engineers must write clear and comprehensible evaluation reports and detailed work orders for the installation crew (engineering technicians/construction engineers). To be a special services engineer, you must have considerable experience with test and maintenance procedures for several kinds of broadcast-related equipment.

"You can learn a lot in a job like this," notes a network engineer. "The pace is fast, you handle a lot of different kinds of jobs on all kinds of systems. But after a while, you may get hungry for a long-term in-depth project. At least I did, so I moved into the audio/video design engineering group where the projects are much more involved, much larger and more complex."

To qualify for this position, your previous experience does not necessarily have to be in television. Working for a manufacturer of television or communications equipment used in television can qualify you, as can military experience as a test engineer in communications.

Where to Apply

Send your resume to the supervisor of special services at NBC network or systems services at CBS. As of this writing, ABC network does not have such a group.

Audio/Video Design Engineer

This engineer is responsible for the design and installation of electronic equipment for all aspects of television production. As with the special/systems services engineering positions, this job requires a broad-based knowledge of television systems design, drafting methods, and the process involved in managing projects. You should have considerable experience in test and maintenance of broadcast communications equipment and the ability to work on very large projects that may take months to complete.

At a network and some specialized production houses, an audio/video design engineer handles the design of multimillion-dollar state-of-the-art edit suites. At a smaller station, the equipment is less sophisticated and the engineer is involved in all aspects of any design and installation project. At a network the engineer assigns tasks—wiring and installation, drafting of blue prints—to support staff. At a smaller station, the projects are smaller and the engineer's responsibility for them greater.

Where to Apply

For a network position, write to the director of the audio/video engineering department or broadcast systems engineering. For a position in a smaller market, contact the person in charge of engineering, sometimes called the chief engineer or engineering supervisor.

MANAGEMENT CAREERS

As an engineer, what do you do after you've made it to the audio/video design engineer level? You could attain the network position of research and development engineer, right at the cutting edge of new technological developments, or you could pursue a managerial career.

With a solid background in television engineering, you could move into project management, responsible for all aspects of a large project, including the financial. Working for you would be a team of other audio/video design engineers.

From that point on, political and corporate considerations enter the picture. However, your best bet for a managerial career is to pick up as much information and experience as you can in each position you hold.

For example, if you are a maintenance engineer, try to get experience both in studio and on-location taping, both live and prerecorded. Before you try to transfer into another department, try to work as a technical supervisor in the field and in the studio. That way you will have solid understanding of the operations. Operations, after all, is your client department and the more you know about operations, the more you have to offer as a manager.

HOW TO GET A JOB

Job Opening: Manager, electronic maintenance.

Job Description: Provide management supervision and direction for electronic maintenance technicians. Provide liaison with other operating areas or division management. Coordinate and work with electronic maintenance management to follow up complaints, job progress, and preventative maintenance. Handle routine daily operations, requests, inquiries, and personnel matters. Obtain and analyze statistical service data. Prepare reports and maintain records.

Requirements: Significant broadcast supervisory or management experience. Excellent interpersonal skills. Ability to organize and maintain progress of multiple projects. Knowledge of application and operation of all types of broadcasting equipment preferred. Technical school graduate with considerable hands-on experience in servicing electronic and electromechanical equipment.

Job Opening: Director of Broadcast Systems Engineering.

Job Description: Direct the design, installation, and implementation of new broadcast related technical systems and facilities. Provide technical guidance and information to aid managers in technical decisions involving broadcast systems. Consult with directors and/or managers of facilities, administration, architectural, construction, air conditioning, technical development, allocations, engineering, and maintenance of all technical design efforts.

Requirements: Considerable management experience with technical personnel and projects. Substantial experience with broadcast systems through maintenance and design. BS Electrical Engineering, required. MS Electrical Engineering or MBA preferred.

These job descriptions are based on actual network job postings. They are typical of those you are likely to see when job hunting. Although Chapter 2 covers topics such as your resume, interviews, and job preparation advice, here are a few guidelines specifically for television engineers:

- Know your equipment. You should know as much as possible about the types of equipment used in television. To stay on top of technological changes, constantly read about engineering from magazines like *Broadcast Engineering, BM/E (Broadcast Management/Engineering), Television Broadcast, Millimeter,* and *Video Systems.*

  Study the job listings in the back of these magazines, not only to find out what jobs are available but to find out what employers are looking for in a candidate.

- Join professional associations such as the Institute of Electrical and Electronics Engineers, Inc. (IEEE), Society of Motion Picture and Television Engineers (SMPTE), and the National Association of Broadcasters (NAB), for publications, information, seminars and other services.
- Read equipment advertisements from the manufacturers. Send away for brochures.
- Do research on the kind of systems and equipment that television stations in your area are using. Phone the engineering department and ask questions. Be extra polite. Often a secretary or a union supervisor will be helpful and informative.

TRAINING AND EDUCATION

Because engineering is a technical profession, technical training is critical. A Bachelor's of Science in electrical engineering (BSEE) from a four-year college is preferable. Computer science courses are useful because computerized equipment is used extensively in television. As a BSEE graduate from a good school, you may find yourself in the pleasant situation of being wooed by multiple system operators eager to find well-educated engineers interested in working in television rather than manufacturing.

A second choice is a two-year technical degree from a junior college with a major in electronics or electrical engineering. A third choice is a degree from a technical high school.

Work/Internship Experience/Vendor Schools

Any television production internships are helpful, but working for a radio station can also be useful preparation. Experience as an audio engineer in a radio station can readily qualify you for an audio engineering position in television production.

Vendor-sponsored training schools are particularly good ways to get experience if you can't get experience on the job. See Chapter 2 for more information about internships and vendor schools.

Experience in Manufacturing

A good preparation for a television career is experience working for manufacturers of communication equipment. Experience in manufacturing and service of any television communication equipment can be extremely valuable to a network.

Licenses and Registration

As a television engineer you may need a first or second class radio-telephone license from the Federal Communications Commission. As an engineer in industry—if you choose to work in industry before you work in television—you may need registration (or licensing) with a professional organization. Licensing and registration is a matter of passing a test designed to show your competency as an engineer. Your local chapter of IEEE or your college engineering department has more information on where and when you can take these tests, how to prepare for them, and whether you need them at all.

RESUME AND INTERVIEW

It's true for all fields, but perhaps more so for a technical one like engineering: keep your resume clear, informative, up-to-date, and brief. Be specific about your experience. With each job description, clearly state what equipment you handled and in what capacity. Don't underplay your technical knowledge and don't exaggerate, either.

If you are just starting out, include any and all television experience—paid or unpaid—in your resume. Also include your grade point average and the titles of any television or engineering courses you have taken, either at school or an adult education, technical, or manufacturer's training school.

Include in your resume those hobbies or interests that relate to engineering, such as ham radio, building electronic kits, working on your stereo.

When you interview for an engineering position, expect to be asked both technical and general questions. As a rule of thumb, the higher the level of your interviewer, the less technical it will be. The higher level interviewers assume you know your technology or you wouldn't have made it that far in the hiring process. The lower level interviewers will be more interested in your technical aptitude and experience.

If you are applying for an entry-level position, such as tape librarian, production assistant, or intern, the interview will be less technical and more personal. After all, you are not expected to know a lot about television at that point. The interviewer will be looking for signs of your energy, enthusiasm, and dedication. Are you the kind of person willing to put in long hours if necessary; are you well organized; do you work well under deadline pressure?

Interviews for technical jobs, such as maintenance, are likely to feature more technical questions. For a videotape maintenance job, for example, a network interviewer asked one applicant: "What would you do if a videotape operator complains that the one tape plays well in one machine and poorly—with picture distortion—in another?"

If your resume indicates strong experience, the interviewer may accept as a given that you understand the basics. "Questions may be very general," says a network maintenance engineer, "and the interviewer may be looking for signs that you understand the lingo. The rest of the emphasis is on personality."

For a design engineering position, technical questions may be more systems-oriented and there may be general questions about fiber optics, satellite, and other high technologies. Your interviewer will want to know how much you understand about the way individual pieces of equipment interact with each other and how you would attack certain systems problems.

"When I applied for a special services engineering position, the interviewer asked me hypothetical questions. He described a scenario and asked me what I would do in that situation," says a network design engineer. "Basically they want to know that if, say, an editing system isn't working, you will know how to figure out where and why. They want to know if you understand how equipment 'talks' to each other."

Whether your interview is technically-oriented or more

personal, try to give examples. Anecdotes are ideal for showing the kind of person and employee you are and demonstrate what you have to offer a team. One network manager suggests that you also bring drawings and photos of systems you have designed. Keep photographic records of the systems you have designed.

UNIONS

As a television engineer, you may be represented by the National Association of Broadcast Employees and Technicians AFL-CIO (NABET) or the International Brotherhood of Electrical Workers (IBEW). Larger stations tend to be unionized. The smaller stations, most public and cable stations, production houses and corporate television departments are nonunion.

The advantages of a union environment include higher salaries, paid overtime (and in television engineering that can add up to a significant amount of money), special rates for working holidays, and job security (it is difficult to get fired or laid off if you are a member of a strong union).

The advantages of a nonunion environment include the less rigid definitions of jobs. In a nonunion environment as an engineer or as a production assistant, you can get hands-on experience with a variety of machinery in a variety of capacities. In contrast, in a union shop there are strict rules about who can touch what equipment and to what extent.

The union situations at the three major networks are very different. At NBC most engineers are members of NABET. At ABC and CBS, the audio/video design engineers are considered members of management and are nonunion. However, the maintenance engineers and equipment operators are union members (NABET). Because the union rules state that management cannot touch equipment, the audio/video design engineers must perform their jobs without physically handling equipment. Instead, they have to point and ask a maintenance person or an operator to push button X and move Part Y when trying to analyze a systems problem.

While these union rules protect jobs, they also create challenges for the manager who enjoys hands-on work. Says a network audio/video design engineer: "By not being allowed to touch equipment, it takes me more time to figure out any systems problems. It would also be much more satisfying if I could play with the system after the project is completed."

FUTURE TRENDS

Will the rapid pace of technological change affect television engineering careers? The answer is yes, and as one network engineer puts it, "That's what keeps the field exciting."

Every year new types of hardware, new ways to transmit television signals, new enhancements such as stereo audio and high definition television are developed. Digital systems are replacing the traditional analog methods, coax cable is being replaced by fiber optics. In addition, there are continual developments in computerized equipment for graphics and special effects, microelectronics are altering the design of entire systems, and advances in satellite transmission are changing the face of broadcasting as we have known it. In 1986, for example, The Center for Advanced Television Studies, an organization established by several leading broadcast companies including ABC, CBS, and 3M Company, awarded its first contract with independent academic institutions for research on ways to improve the U.S. television system.

As a result of ongoing and future efforts to improve television, television engineers are becoming more than just electrical engineers. In the next decade, more computer engineers, telecommunications engineers, and field engineers will understand the use of satellite transmission or the interactive systems that let field engineers transmit signals directly to the station from a cable subscriber's home set.

The number of television engineers may remain stable despite the changing technologies, because, while some changes reduce the required number of engineers, others may create enough new jobs to offset the loss. New technologies like videotex, teletext, interactive video discs, stereo sound, computerized newsrooms, and new videotape formats may modify current jobs as well as create new opportunities for television engineers.

As an engineer, what should you do in the face of all this change? "You must keep up with it all by reading the trade magazines and attending conferences whenever possible," advises a network engineer. "And try to get as much training as possible. If you are working in a network or a large station that has a training department, ask about courses that you can take to keep you informed. Vendor courses can be excellent."

If you are working in a smaller station that is group owned, check with your manager to see if the parent company offers training opportunities. Find out about vendor training opportunities. If you can't get your station to pay for the training, use your vacation or take a leave of absence and go on your own.

A Talk With . . .

Joe Berini
Vice President, Engineering, KRON-TV, Chronicle Broadcasting Company, San Francisco

> *Joe Berini began his career in television as an electronic technician. Today he is responsible for KRON's engineering department and those of Chronicle Broadcasting's other stations as well. Berini oversees the company-wide purchasing of engineering equipment, acts both as a consultant to the individual stations and acts as chief engineer at KRON. As he puts it: "It makes for a very long day." Key to Berini's career path was his early interest in the engineering behind news production (electronic journalism) and its portable equipment. At one point he used to have a sign over his desk that read: "Toy Televisions Fixed Here."*

I had been an electronic technician in the Coast Guard. So, when I came home, I got a job as a maintenance engineer in the local TV station in Duluth. I worked the evening shift so that I could go to school during the day. [He earned a BA in psychology with a minor in communications.]

As a maintenance engineer in a small station, I did more than maintain equipment. I did just about everything except sell time. I ran master control, camera, videotape, audio, and I switched. After I graduated from college, I began my Masters [in communications, with a minor in psychology] and, meanwhile, worked at the station as a news director for the evening news.

Later on I went to Saudi Arabia for a year and a half as a broadcast engineer for Aramco, an oil company that owned an English language TV station. Basically, I maintained the station for them—I was the only Western engineer there, and I also trained Arabs in maintenance and operations. It was tough there—no women and no alcohol . . .

My next move was back to the States where I settled down in San Francisco. I got a job at the CBS affiliate there as a maintenance engineer. Later I became crew chief for maintenance working on small field ENG [electronic news gathering] equipment. I got that job because nobody else wanted it. But I had a feeling that small ENG equipment was the way of the future. And my guess paid off. I worked there for three and a half years and then moved to KRON where I soon became associate news director of engineering.

I love what I do. The business is so fascinating. I come in in the morning and never know what's going to happen. Just keeping up with the technology is the biggest job I have. New technology breaks in the news side of television production before it does in other areas. For instance, we were the first station to get into KU band satellite technology—trucks (called portable uplinks) that transmit signals to satellites so that we can broadcast live from almost anywhere in the world.

The hardest thing for me about my television career is that I don't spend the time I'd like with my family. But it's worth it—if it weren't I wouldn't be doing it. Instead, I try to make my time at home "quality time."

Advice

When people call me about getting into television, I say go to Fresno or New Rochelle—a small place where you can learn a lot. The most valuable experience I've had is learning the whole gamut. It helped me understand what you can do with technology and how it can be used. That's where engineering gets creative.

Jack Davis
Director of Engineering, Meyer Television Network, North Dakota

> *Jack Davis is responsible for the purchase, operation, and maintenance of the broadcast equipment at four television stations in North Dakota. He began his television career as a transmitter operator in Fargo, North Dakota. He then moved up the engineering ladder to maintenance technician, studio supervisor, chief engineer, and now director. Through his various positions and over 20 years, Davis has maintained equipment, supervised major renovation projects, and built new facilities, including one of the four stations he directs.*

I was originally attracted to the television business because of a mistaken impression I had—namely, that television is glamorous. Actually, TV is glamorous, but then I discovered that my particular end of it isn't. Once the aura of TV wore off, I found that engineering was a lot more stimulating than I thought, and I was motivated to stay for other reasons. Engineering is technically challenging, and I'm working with an ever-changing technology.

I got my initial training at a two-year trade school. I did well because technical things come kind of easy for me. I was also very introverted at the time, and my first television job was perfect for me. I was a transmitter operator sitting underneath a 2,060 foot tower about 55 miles away from town. It was very isolated. The only people I saw were the guy I relieved when I came on duty and the guy who replaced me. Then I got drafted into the army, where as an introvert I ended up with very little. So, I managed to change my personality and became much more outgoing. When I came back home to the transmitter, the isolation made me crazy.

So, as soon as there was an opening at the television studio, I changed positions.

I like what I've been doing. Not having a tremendous amount of formal education, I've always trained myself. I get a project, go ahead and do it. When I solve rather complex problems, I feel very good.

I work long hours, but I don't blame the business for that. I'm basically a workaholic, so that's my problem. However, I do develop a certain amount of gratification from sitting at home and seeing that everything is working. And I like turning the channel selector and seeing that mine looks better than theirs . . . A friend of mine once said that being a television engineer is like wetting yourself in a dark suit. You get a nice warm feeling but nobody notices. A sign that I'm doing my job is that nothing goes wrong. When nothing goes wrong, nobody notices.

Advice

I think TV is a real dynamic field for someone who has the desire. That's what you have to have—a little desire. It helps to be curious. You just need general electronics training . . . When I look at an applicant, I look for a real interest in broadcasting. If a person is a ham radio operator, I know there's a real interest. Most engineers that are good are also hams—it simply stems from performing better in your job if you're interested.

A Talk With . . .
Louis Libin
Manager of Allocation Engineering, NBC-TV

> *Louis Libin is responsible for the licensing of over 200 affiliates, NBC's Owned & Operated stations, and WNBC. The department participates in industry committee work relating to frequency allocations, inspects NBC's owned radio and television stations, as well as the affiliates, and provides engineering guidance to other NBC departments. Libin began his career at NBC as a broadcast systems engineer. Before reaching his current position, he*

was a staff engineer for technical development (research and development).

I hadn't planned on a career in television at all. While studying physics and electronic engineering in college, I worked during the day at Burroughs Computers as a field engineer. Then one spring, on impulse I stopped in at a job fair at my university. ABC had a table there and was recruiting technicians. After a ten-minute interview, I was told that if I had a valid FCC license, I could start in six weeks. The test required knowledge of electronics—which I had—and of Morse Code, which I had learned as a hobbyist. So I took the test to get my FCC license and started at ABC as a broadcast technician six weeks later.

I started that first job at ABC with very little applied knowledge. I'd never before seen a vectorscope or a waveform monitor; however, within a month I was heavily involved with video equipment in ABC's Technical Operation Center. It was interesting work and I was still in school, but I'm not sure where I was learning more. I decided, though, to get some solid experience in television from the manufacturing side and accepted a job offer from Chyron [manufacturers of television character and special effects generators] as a test/design engineer. After that I went to Loral [a manufacturer of communications and military equipment] and worked as a high-speed video processing design engineer. After a short time there, I was recruited by NBC.

I mostly consider myself an electrical engineer who works in television. I would like to be more aware of the television aspect in addition to the engineering. The more I know about television itself, the more I can contribute. I dislike when people call us "black box" engineers, which implies that we just connect other people's circuits together. That to me isn't engineering . . .

I like what I do for several reasons. I like the pressure of deadlines, of constantly having to maintain signal integrity. We have a network signal going out to the over 200 affiliates every day. And before that signal goes out it has to pass through a lot of processing equipment, cable and airwaves—and no matter what that signal passes through, when it comes out, it has to be as good as when it originated.

Advice

Television engineering has traditionally been a line of work that you didn't need a degree to get into. When someone with an education comes in, he or she can move up very, very quickly. So my first recommendation is to get the best education you can. It doesn't matter what you get your degree in— engineering, journalism, computers, liberal arts. Even if you don't need the degree for the job, you might need it later, and it will give you an advantage over other applicants. Besides, that degree will give you something else you'll need—confidence.

7

Videotape Editors

Television videotape editors are the people responsible for the order in which we see images on the screen. Both film and videotape are used for television programs, but videotape is much more common.

There is, however, much overlap between videotape editing and film editing. Basic concepts of juxtaposing images and the order in which they are placed to tell a story effectively, apply to both media. Despite the technical differences of working with film and videotape, editors are often trained in both media. Career switches between film and television are not uncommon.

The role of a videotape editor varies in television depending upon the producer, the editor, and the relationship between them. An editor's role can range from highly imaginative to merely technical. A creative editor actively shapes a story by choosing where and when to make cuts. A passive editor executes the cuts selected by the producer.

As with most aspects of television production, the larger the station, the more likely it is that the editors will work on highly sophisticated electronic equipment.

In private television, more television/video departments are hiring their own editors (who may have to do other television jobs as well if there isn't enough work for full-time editing), and the level of sophistication is approaching that of broadcasting.

Production houses, whose clients range from advertising to

entertainment to corporate, tend to have network-quality, sophisticated equipment, and network news level deadline pressure. In production houses, however, there is an additional pressure: Editing rooms, because of the cost of their equipment, command high prices for their use ($300 to $500 an hour is not unusual). Therefore, clients particularly appreciate editors who can work quickly and help them make the most of each precious hour.

What personal qualities are required for a television editor? The consensus from editors and those who hire them (usually former editors) is that first you must have a creative eye with an understanding of how pictures tell a story. You also need to thrive under deadline pressure and be willing to work long hours and almost any or all shifts in a 24-hour day. One network news editor called editing "the perfect job for a single, uncommitted person." You must be able to communicate, whether with producers, clients, or corporate executives. You should also understand the subject matter you are editing. In other words, to be a good editor, you have to be, as one network editor put it, "more than a button pusher."

WHAT IS TELEVISION EDITING?

Television editing, like film editing, is the process by which visual images are assembled. Unlike film editing, however, which involves manipulating reels of film, editing videotape is done electronically. Basically, the television editor records on a master tape the portions of the original tape he or she has chosen to tell the story, in the desired order.

At its simplest, videotape editing uses two small videotape player/recorders with which you assemble a "roughcut," the video equivalent of a rough draft. Known as offline editing, this is an economical way of seeing how the finished video would look before committing significant sums of money for the final high-tech edit.

At its most complex, television editing involves rooms full of multimillion dollar equipment capable of dramatic special visual effects, such as wipes (one image replacing another literally as though wiped on), dissolves, split screens, swooping, spinning and flipping images, as well as special audio effects.

While both technical and artistic aspects of editing are essential, as one network editor puts it, "We've found that if a person is creative and has a good eye, we can teach him the equipment. But it doesn't often work the other way around."

Different Programs, Different Editing

While a good editor will be able to edit almost any kind of program, there are significant differences in editing for different kinds of programs. You may find that you are adept at one particular kind, or, even if you can handle all types equally well, you may find you nonetheless prefer working in one area.

News Editing

In television news, an editor works mostly on what are known as "crash and burn" stories—late-breaking stories that must be edited quickly. Editors who work on these stories generally perform "straight cuts" (meaning no special effects) and have a gift for both manual dexterity and the ability to determine quickly which images are essential to tell the story.

Usually by the time the news editor sees the tape to be edited, the producer and writer of the story have already prepared a script. This means the news editor's function is to take the script and select images that work with the script in terms of duration and concept. Sometimes, however, a story is first cut by the editor and a script is written to fit the edited tape. "This often works better," says a network editor. "It's harder work for the editor, but it's often better because the pictures tell the story. The other way, with the editing following a pre-written script, it is easier to edit, but there isn't always a natural visual flow."

Feature, or special segment, editors handle stories two to six-minutes long. Generally these are handled by editors who are particularly creative visually when putting together a story. Since often they have as long as a week to edit a two-minute story, technical speed is less important than their creative eye.

Documentary Editing

Documentaries traditionally were shot on film and transferred onto videotape when used for television airing. Today, however, videotape quality approaches that of film, and more documentaries are shot in this less expensive and easier-to-work-with medium.

Documentary videotape editors, who may work for independent producers or be part of a network documentary unit, often participate in the documentary from the start. The editor's assignment may last anywhere from six weeks to a year. At a network, the assignment may be for a 20-minute segment in a documentary-style news magazine program; an independent production may be for an hour or two-hour special.

The documentary editor is generally considered to be more than a technician. "Producers and directors of documentaries often rely on the editor for creative input. Documentary editing is a highly creative job," says a director of network editing.

Entertainment Editing

Entertainment editors who work on situation comedies, weekly dramas, and other scripted story-programs, generally play a highly creative role and are involved in the program from the beginning, during script development. In this role, the editor contributes to the "look" of the program, the pace of the program, and methods to cut scenes to make the most of the emotional impact.

Production House Editing

As an editor in a production house, your work may include any of the described kinds of editing assignments plus commercials, music videos, or openings for shows. You may also get assignments that require different styles of work. An important aspect of production house editing is client contact.

Production house work entails a certain amount of risk.

"Your job may be here today and gone tomorrow depending on business," says an editor. On the positive side, you can be creative and have access to the latest and equipment. Many networks go to quality production houses for some of their more complicated and fancier editing jobs.

A Day With . . .

The Videotape Editors at a Major Network

What actually goes on every day in a television editing department? First of all, in television editing a day is literally 24 hours. Work is performed around the clock. This is because editing equipment is expensive, and it is a better investment if it is used around the clock.

If you work at a television station and are assigned to work on the morning news program, you can expect a shift that begins at midnight and goes until 8 in the morning. In contrast, on an evening news program, work begins at 10 or 11 AM and goes until air time.

In entertainment or production house work, the patterns are less definable. Entertainment editing at a network may be relegated to the night hours, when edit rooms are more likely to be available. During the day the afternoon and evening news programs are priority. At a production house, you tend to work when the client wants to work. Most often edits are performed until they are completed, and a day's work can go way beyond seven hours. If you work in a production house or in a private television department that does not have its own editing suites, you can expect to work at night and on weekends. Rates are cheaper then, and many clients try to cut costs whenever possible.

What follows is a sample day in the life of two editing departments, showing editing during both daily news production and post-production. While this example is of editing at a major network, local station editing departments and production companies operate similarly, but on a smaller scale and with less predictable routine. In a television network there are many editing rooms operating simultaneously; post-production and daily production occur concurrently.

Midnight

As a news videotape editor assigned to the morning news show, your day begins somewhere between midnight and 2 AM. When you come in, you check your schedule to see what edit room you are assigned to for the morning news show. You also check with your supervisor to find out if there are any emergency stories that you should work on immediately. You set up the edit room and equipment, gathering tapes you need from the videotape library and preparing new tapes for editing by setting color bars and tone. Until 3 AM, this may be a very quiet, slow period.

3 AM

Most satellite feeds from overseas come in around now. These satellite feeds are of news footage from other parts of the world where the day is only now ending. Editors on duty at this hour record these feeds.

Taking in feeds, as this process is called, is a technical process during which you are concerned mostly with picture and sound quality. After the editor has recorded them, some tapes are edited into stories for transmission to affiliate stations, and others are transmitted directly as is.

4 AM

If there is time, you have a lunch break around now.

5 AM

At this point, the pace quickens as preparations for the morning broadcast begin. Stories are completed for the 7 AM broadcast by 6:15. Late breaking news is worked on right up to and even during airtime.

8 to 9 AM

The night crew returns tapes already aired to the library and leaves.

9:30 to 10 AM

The next shift comes in, checks its schedule, and reports to the appropriate edit room. The crew works on advance stories, breaking stories or waits for an assignment. This is a quiet period.

10:30 AM

The editor begins work for the evening news programs. He or she sets up the editing room, turns on editing machines, prepares enough tape for the day by setting bars and tone (pre-marking tapes that will be used by preparing its color and audio levels according to a standard setting).

3 to 4 PM

Satellite feeds start coming in. Work schedule gets hectic with the approach of airtime. Sometimes there is barely enough time to receive a satellite feed and get it onto a play-back machine for broadcast. Most of the work around this time is on the evening news program.

4 PM

The third shift of editors comes in. They work until about midnight. They set up their materials and work on stories for the morning news and advance items such as feature stories, documentaries, and other nonbreaking news.

5 PM

As many as fifteen stories may be in the editing process at this time. This can be a very tense time as editors, producers, and writers race against the clock.

6:15 PM

Ideally, all stories for the 7 PM news are ready by now. How-ever, late-breaking stories or problems with satellite feeds may mean that editors are still working on stories.

6:30 PM

Taping begins on the evening news, though it may not be aired until half an hour later in many markets. Editors working on late-breaking stories may still be working—obviously un-der extreme pressure. No one can afford to talk in full sen-tences any more. There is total concentration on getting the job done.

7 PM

Broadcast for evening news. Many crew members (except for those who are jaded or are still editing) watch the broadcast to see how the show looks. Errors noticed can be changed for later feeds to network affiliates in other time zones.

8 PM

With the evening news broadcast over, editors on the evening shift (4 PM to Midnight), continue editing documentaries and features as well as news stories for the next day's morning news program. These editors work on entertainment and other programs as well.

Meanwhile, Back at the Post-Production Department . . .

Editing is going on throughout the day and night along with post-production editing. Beginning at about 8 AM, the post-production crew (editor, audio engineer, and assistant editor) set up the room for their shift of work: gathering tapes, preparing tapes for editing, and general organization of elements (such as graphics) to be used during the day's editing sessions.

By 9 AM, together with the producer the post-production editing crew begins work. Assignments may be to select sections from many tapes brought in from the field or shot in studios to assemble a rough cut, or combine segments that are already edited.

Basically, the concern throughout the day is what the next shot is and how the transition will be made. "Order and transitions. That's all we do," says a network post-production editor. The process continues either until the job is completed or, if the deadline is not imminent, until everyone has had enough and before too much costly overtime is incurred.

Post-production often goes on throughout the evening and into the wee hours. Since news programs and promotion have priority on the post-production crews and edit rooms, much of the daytime work is devoted to them. Entertainment editing therefore can get bumped to the less amenable hours between midnight and 8 AM.

CAREER PATH FOR TELEVISION VIDEOTAPE EDITORS

Once you get your foot in the door, expect to learn on the job and get the training you need to rise to assistant editor and editor.

In many ways, the editing career path is marked by greater mastery of more sophisticated equipment. For this reason, reaching the network level is often a career goal itself. What follows is a list of jobs in order of increasing experience.

Production Assistant, Intern, Secretary and Other Entry-Level Jobs

For information about these jobs, see Chapter 2. Whatever the entry-level job, make your editing interests known and you may get a chance to work in the editing room with the editor—even if only as a gofer.

Researcher/Videotape Library

Researcher/Videotape Library is an entry-level position where you can gain contact with the editing department at a network. Small stations, corporate departments and production houses are not likely to have this position since the scope of their activity is generally not large enough to warrant it.

You will work with editors every day, bring tapes they need, and file those they have finished. A network news editor supervisor says: "It might enable you to get a chance for training as an assistant editor during vacation relief period."

Where to Apply

Contact large television stations and networks and find out the name of the supervisor of the videotape research library. Send your resume and a cover letter to that person.

Assistant Editor/Videotape Operator

The closest position to an editor-in-training is the post of assistant editor. This position is sometimes also called videotape operator because the job may involve operating the videotape player/recorder for the editor while the editor manipulates other equipment or makes decisions. Videotape operators can also be nothing more than operators, but you can often turn it into an assistant editor position by showing initiative.

The only requirement for this position is that you be able to prepare tapes for editing by recording color bars and tone on the tapes so that they are in "tune." This requires knowing how to read and analyze a basic video signal on a waveform monitor and vectorscope and knowing how to describe components of that signal and break them down to make sure the video and audio signal is without distortion.

In corporate television or a production house, the assistant editor also performs such tasks as loading videotapes, preparing them for editing (setting color bars and tone), viewing them and "pulling selects"—looking for sections that are appropriate for a program.

As an assistant editor you may also assemble the rough cuts. After the selects are approved and their order of appearance roughly determined, you may rough out the program using a basic editing machine and record the selected segments in their proper order, marking where a graphic occurs or the narrator appears (if not already taped). Your job also includes participation during the on-line or final edit, which takes place in the multimillion dollar editing suite and includes the assembly of graphics, music, and final audio.

During on-line editing, your role is most likely to load the source tapes (those containing the original raw footage) needed during the edit. This is a job best characterized as hyperactive if the edit involves many different original tapes not used in sequence. Or, it can involve a lot of sitting on a couch in the edit room during which you can analyze the decisions the editor is making, daydream, or goof around. (Goofing around is an important and frequent antidote to the high pressure of television work; when there is free time, it is important to take advantage of it.)

Where to Apply

To apply for an assistant editor/videotape operator position, you must have some prior experience in television, either as a production assistant or researcher, or have training on the basic editing equipment. Usually someone already on staff is promoted and given on-the-job training. However, you can occasionally enter at this level. Your best bet is to contact the manager of post-production at television stations and production houses. In corporate television departments, contact the department manager.

Vacation Relief Editor

An institution almost exclusive to networks is the vacation relief system. During a time period that can range from two to six months, the networks often hire temporary editors to fill in for editors who are on vacation.

These job positions are for a specified length of time, but if you do well your employment may be extended. Generally you must be experienced as an editor to get a vacation relief position, but sometimes a network department may save a few spaces for people with little experience in television who have a good background in the visual arts. First crack at these coveted training positions may go to insiders—usually assistant editors or tape operators on staff—but there may be spaces left for outsiders. At NBC in New York City, these lucky few may get as much as five weeks of training and some limited opportunities to edit shows.

Where to Apply

To apply for vacation relief jobs, contact the editing departments of major networks and the larger affiliate and independent stations. The most important factor in applying for these posts is timing. It is critical to call and find out when vacation relief is at that station and when the supervisor of editing prefers to receive resumes. Never send a reel unless you have permission.

Videotape Editor ―――――――――――――――――――――

A position as an editor requires previous experience as an assistant editor, training on basic equipment through one of the manufacturer's training schools, or vacation relief experience.

Experience as a film editor can also qualify you for a position as a television editor. In fact, film editors are sometimes highly prized, despite their lack of technical expertise in the videotape medium. They "are very talented at editing from a creative point of view because they spent more time doing the creative work and less learning how to operate technical equipment," notes a network director.

Film editors are particularly useful in dramas and made-for-television movies. Many professionals are looking to hire people with proven creative talent for putting images together; they feel that they can teach them the technological skills.

If you begin in news, which involves straight cutting and a lot of it, you can hone your skills quickly. You may also start in a production house or a corporate video department. Whenever you work, however, you can always choose to move into an area that suits you best. Some editors thrive on the fast pace and the deadline pressure of news; others are better suited for longer-term projects. Some positions require mastery of more sophisticated equipment, but it's difficult to say one position is higher than another; it's a question of taste.

Where to Apply

Send your resume and cover letter directly to the director of editing. It helps to know when people are hiring, so do some sleuthing. Often secretaries or assistants can be informative.

Read the trade papers and industry newsletters. If you hear someone in editing has been promoted, that usually has a trickledown effect, and slots beneath will open up. One of those may be right for you (and vice versa). Do not send your reel unless you have permission.

Post-Production Videotape Editor ―――――――――

While being an editor is a career in itself, being a post-production editor is a logical next step. Post-production editors perform on-line edits (final edits) using sophisticated equipment for special effects—ADO, Quantel, Dubner, Mirage, and others. (See page 217 for more information about these machines.)

The role of a post-production editor is, as one network editor explains, "to create the desired visual effect, cutting not only for content, but for impact."

Where to Apply

Post-production jobs are generally the exclusive domain of large well-equipped stations, corporate television studios and production houses. The prerequisite is significant editing experience and familiarity with at least some of the equipment involved. You may find that becoming adept at one particular piece of equipment is helpful in terms of moving into post-production. Apply to the manager of post-production at a network station. When applying to production houses, call first and find out who makes the decisions to hire editors. Often, your best bet is to get your post-production experience at a place where you are already an editor. From there you can apply for post-production work elsewhere.

LIFE AFTER EDITING

If it turns out that editing alone is not the lifetime career for you, you might move on to:

- *Producing:* Creative editors often move into producing. If that is your ultimate goal, it is important to develop yourself to be a creative editor rather than a technical one.
- *Managing:* Editors can also move into management beginning by supervising editors—hiring and firing, disciplining, rewarding, scheduling, and training them to keep them at their maximum potential. Managing can branch off into keeping a facility up to date and making decisions about new equipment and incorporating the old.

    If you learn about other technical aspects of broadcasting in addition to editing, you could qualify for broadcast control manager, responsible for scheduling both people and facilities involved in transmission of programming and newsfeeds. You might also qualify for a directorship in charge of editing and other technical matters for all the affiliates of a network or a group of stations owned by one company.

HOW TO GET A JOB

Here are our conclusions based on interviews with professionals about the training needed to become a videotape editor, what managers look for, and what should be on your resume and reel. The basics of how to get a television production job are covered in Chapter 2.

TRAINING AND EDUCATION

". . . Training is one of the most difficult things in the editing business. We have very few places available in the major markets," says a director of network editing.

Most editors, therefore, recommend that you get training from the manufacturers of editing equipment. Known in the trade as vendor schools, these training classes are often reasonably priced because they are part of the manufacturer's promotional/sales efforts.

Sony, CMX, and Convergence offer training on their equipment, as do many other companies. In order to find out about vendor training opportunities, read the trade papers and write to the manufacturers of the equipment you are interested in mastering. (Also, see the list of vendor schools in the Appendix.)

Contact professional organizations, talk to teachers at school or professionals you know, and ask for suggestions. Find out what equipment a local station you want to work for uses, and try to get training on that brand and type.

You should have at least a Bachelor's degree from an

accredited college or university. Degrees in the arts or journalism are preferred. Photography or film degrees indicate that you have a certain amount of visual knowledge and experience.

A journalism degree is useful for news positions and corporate jobs (corporate departments treat much of their programming as news programming). It indicates that you understand the fundamentals of the business and will be able to work with journalists. "Generally we hire only editors who have a degree in journalism or the arts. They must have the background to understand what it takes to write and produce a news story," says a director of network editing.

Basically, get any kind of television experience and training you can, preferably before you finish college. If you have no other options, take courses in television production in schools of continuing education. Even if the courses are not on a network or local production level, you will at least get a taste of television and you may meet people who can help you with contacts.

RESUME AND REEL

See Chapter 2 for information about preparing a resume and reel. Try to get across the creative role you may have played in any work you have done, even if you are applying for a technical position. You are competing against many others; anything that will make you stand out and show you have potential to grow beyond a technical job can give you a competitive edge. Most managers are interested in your reel, but not until they ask for it.

Managers are not likely to view your cassette without you because they want to know your contribution to the editing. "People always look at reels a little skeptically because sometimes you can have three people walk in with the same reel. Nothing turns a person off faster than an applicant who shows a very elaborate reel and is then vague about his contribution," explains one network editor.

UNIONS

If you work as a videotape editor in a union environment, you will most likely become a member of NABET, the National Association of Broadcast Employees and Technicians. Most union shops are in larger stations and in major networks.

Union membership is mandatory in a union shop. Becoming a member is simply a matter of getting a job at a unionized station and paying a one-time initiation fee and regular dues.

As a member of the union, your salary, raises, vacation time and other benefits will be negotiated for you, but you can negotiate your salary level (generally based on number of years of experience) and bargain for a higher paying level.

Working in a union shop gives you protection regarding job security and benefits, and strict rules about overtime pay—to your benefit, considering the amount of overtime editors usually have to perform. However, strict job descriptions make it more difficult for beginners to get involved in a wide range of work at a television station.

These strict union work rules are designed to protect the worker from being asked to do the work of a higher paid employee without getting commensurate pay. However, for a production assistant who would relish the hands-on opportunities despite the lack of pay, some union rules are disadvantageous.

Most production companies are nonunion as are many small stations and corporate television departments. The highest pay scales are found in production companies but are reserved for editors who have proven themselves extremely valuable as client pleasers. Production house pay can range from half of its network equivalent to many times more than network scale in the case of "star" quality editors.

FUTURE TRENDS

With the continual improvement and enhancement of television editing technology, editors must constantly learn and master new equipment. However, this does not occur at a frantic pace because the cost of editing equipment prevents many stations and production houses from discarding older equipment.

While it is difficult to predict the future of television editing, it is likely that fewer editors will be necessary as more and more equipment is automated. Ideally, however, this will be offset by an increase in programming.

As the equipment is made more "user friendly," editors need less technical aptitude and more creative talent. The emphasis in the future may be towards editor/producers—editors who are as involved in the content of the program they are cutting as they are in the individual cuts.

A Talk With . . .
Bobby Lee Lawrence
General Manager, News Engineering and
Electronic Journalism, NBC News

> *Bobby Lee Lawrence supervises a worldwide engineering staff responsible for covering both planned and breaking news stories. Under his supervision are also approximately 80 staff editors who edit NBC's network news programs. Lawrence describes his editors as being "uniquely talented to deal with quick news cutting" for breaking news. The department, which works round the clock, also handles post production for several other NBC-TV shows including the magazine 1986, religious documentaries, NBC News White Papers and the children's show Main Street.*

"Although my training and college degree were related to business, I started out working within an electronic environment. Then I became involved in radar system technology and worked as an electronic radar repairman following post grad electronics training. I became interested in television technology as an engineer and started working for a manufacturer of videotape editing systems. I headed up their field service department and traveled around the world training editors in computerized editing.

I also worked [for the editing system manufacturer] as a consultant in building studios and post production facilities and spent time editing documentaries and commercials in the Los Angeles area. I was senior technical adviser there when I was approached by NBC Network to train their editors to understand the marriage between the creative and technical sides of videotape editing.

I really enjoy my job. News is an exciting business and I enjoy the excitement. It's very difficult not to become excited at the opportunity of seeing pictures of the news before they are presented to the world. You're putting together a package to present to the world, hopefully not biased. When you see your product on national TV you have an enormous sense of pride and accomplishment.

NBC Network has given me the opportunity to advance along a career path that best suits my talents. Working in news is unpredictable and will test your mettle over and over again. When a company recognizes hard work and dedication, you feel that your career choice was the right one.

I also enjoy the interplay among the people who are producing the information and matching the video and sound to present in an interesting format. Every time you cut a story you are thinking about how people are going to receive that information . . . And, how well can I cut this story? Can I do better than any one else? Being egotistical is part of being a videotape editor. Cutting a story and having it aired is what it's all about."

A Talk With . . .

Kirk Daniels
Chief Videotape Editor, WTEN-TV,
Albany, New York.

> *As chief videotape editor in a 50th market station,*
> *Daniels is responsible for the editing of commercials*
> *for local advertisers, specials, and some news.*

I started at WTEN fresh out of high school, working part-time while I was in junior college. I got the job through my guidance counselor at college and started doing operations—running videotape, running camera, doing master control switching, and running an audio board. In 1970, when I graduated—I got my degree in electronic engineering technology—I came to work at Channel 10 full time.

As the years progressed, I became stronger in one field— videotape editing. At one point I went to New York City for a week-long seminar on computerized editing through Convergence Technology [a leading manufacturer of television editing equipment] and was trained by one of the top editors in the country—an editor who has edited *Barney Miller* and has worked with Francis Ford Coppola.

I find editing fascinating. There's never a dull moment. Every project has a challenge and I try to meet it. If I can't meet that challenge, it's time for me to get out of the business. Broadcasting is a growing business, there are a lot of avenues to be turned . . .

I like working in this size market. I could become an editor in New York City, but I don't want to get tied into one operation. I like the versatility here. I like to get my hands on other things, not just editing. In big markets you're confined to one basic operation."

Advice

I think students should start as early as possible. They should go to college and get a maintenance training program. It's very important that they know their electronic background. Then they can come and get on-the-job training to operate. As the technologies change, it's vitally important to get into the electronic background of it. You should know how to program the computers used [in production equipment]—you should know how the equipment works, not just how to work the equipment . . ."

A Talk With . . .

Gary Brasher
Chief CMX Editor and Operations Manager,
California Video Center, Los Angeles

> *Gary Brasher has edited* Falcon Crest, The Tonight
> Show *anniversary shows, NBC-TV network promotional*

material, and many game shows including The All New
Let's Make a Deal, Love Connection, *and* The Million
Dollar Chance of a Lifetime. *A totally self-taught editor,
Brasher learned how to do Convergence and CMX editing by studying the manual and its diagrams. His non-
editing credits include producing* PM Magazine, *directing the broadcasts of Baltimore Orioles baseball games,
directing newscasts, and shooting camera for newscasts,
football game coverage, and commercials. An interview
with him covering his producing and directing experience appears on page 115.*

I majored in television at the University of Houston—that's
how I got my entree into the television business. My first job
was in 1971 at KVOA-TV in Tucson, Arizona, where I worked
as a part-time studio cameraman the summer between my
sophomore and junior years of college.

I ran camera there for the summer and returned to school.
Then, one day, I had an appointment with one of my profes-
sors. I was waiting outside his door and he was talking to one
of his, well, teacher's pets. He told that person that there's a
new TV station opening up in town called Channel 26 and
they are looking for a studio camera person. As soon as I
heard that I immediately ran over to my car and drove there
and told them my professor told me to apply for the job. So
they gave me the job. I was in the right place at the right
time . . . That's how I snuck my way into working for a TV
station in Houston.

I got into editing much later. After I'd been producing *PM
Magazine* [WCMH-TV, Ohio] for eight months, I got a phone
call from a friend in San Francisco who was working with the
creator of *PM,* Bill Hillier. Hillier was now starting up a nation-
ally-syndicated program *The World of People* and was looking
for a director. Although I was called the director, I was actually the supervisor of the staff of editors who edited segments
for the magazine-style show. My job was also to edit together
the segments and integrate them into the final show. I used
the Convergence editing system for that show. I didn't go to
any school to learn how. I simply looked at the machine, read
the manual and did it . . .

When the show was cancelled a year later, all the equipment
used in the show was sold. The company that bought the edit

bay I was working in called and said: "Help! We need someone to show us how to run it." That's how I started as a
freelance video editor . . .

I enjoy editing because you have an opportunity to take a lot
of unrelated pieces of material and put them together in a
way that tells a story, brings order to the confusion. Editing
takes the essence and puts it on the screen in such a way that
people can understand the story and enjoy what they see. I
get a real sense of accomplishment from it. It's like starting
with a pile of sand and building a sand castle.

Advice

If you want to get into the TV business, don't be afraid to take
any job that is offered to you no matter how menial it may
sound. The way to success in this business is by hard work
and never saying no. If someone wants to hire you to sweep
floors, take the job, sweep the floor and work your way up.

8

Graphic Artists

"I get asked all the time what television graphic artists do," a designer on a local television news show laments. "My answer is usually: You know the little box that's just over the shoulder of the reporter or anchor? I make the stuff that goes in that box."

While the bulk of television news graphics is what appears in the box over a reporter's shoulder, television graphics as a whole covers far more ground.

Whether the show is a documentary, news, sports, a corporate television show, a weekly situation comedy, or the latest mini-series, graphic artists are responsible for the opening graphics, the titles, the "bumper" (the display with the show's title that tells you "we will return in a moment after these messages"), illustrations to explain a complex financial or scientific subject, television station logos, and others.

At their simplest, television graphics provide the viewer with an easy-to-read visual aid that identifies the subject of the program being shown. At their most complex, they are pyrotechnical displays of swooping, spinning, splashing, and exploding configurations cooked up by today's computer graphics. You've probably seen the effects of computer graphics in the latest station identifications of the networks, not to mention the extravaganzas that now illustrate major election coverage. The days of simple bar charts are gone.

As an artist, your career opportunities in television range from cut-and-paste art to illustration with electronic paint systems or computer graphics.

Whether you are considering a career in television computer graphics, animation, or hand-made illustration, there are three principles you should bear in mind as you read this chapter:

- Regardless of the technology you choose—the hand or the computer—you must have good basic design sense.
- While it is not a requirement, it helps enormously to be well informed about the kind of programming you choose to illustrate.
- As with almost any job in television, you should be willing, able and even eager to work under severe deadline pressure, especially, but not exclusively, in television news.

WHAT IS TELEVISION GRAPHICS?

"Hours of labor, seconds of glory." For many television graphics people, this is their working slogan. Except perhaps for the openings and closings of regularly scheduled shows, much of television graphics is on the air for only a few seconds. However, as brief as five seconds is, in television time that is long enough to do the job: to communicate.

Turn on your television set and watch a news program. You will see as many as three basic kinds of graphics (all of which apply to other types of programming as well):

- Story illustrations in the box over anchor/reporter's shoulder.
- Animated opening, closing, and "bumpers" before commercial breaks.
- Animated illustrations of a complex concept.

Much of your work is comparable to that of an advertising graphic artist. As in advertising, TV graphic design has to work symbolically. "You need good, strong, clean design, almost like package design," a network art director explains, "because television can't handle fancy subtleties. It's like walking down the aisle in a supermarket—the viewer/consumer has to be able to know that a red can means cola and a green can means ginger ale. TV graphic design has to be that strong, so strong that it can tell you what the story is about—even without the slug [the caption]."

"We don't have the luxury of a newspaper or magazine where a person can look through the pages and say, hey that's a beautiful illustration," the network director continues. "In television you're talking about a five-second graphic that has to be clear enough that it doesn't distract the viewer from what the reporter or narrator is saying, yet bold enough that it will be noticed."

While the function of a graphic is basic, its execution can vary from high tech to handmade. Which method will be used depends on time, personnel available, and most important, the level of equipment at the station.

Take a story called "Lebanon in Crisis." At a local station, a graphic illustrating it might show a torn Lebanese flag with the story's name in a caption. The artist might buy a postcard of the Lebanese flag (20 cents at the United Nations), cut a jagged line down the middle, lay blue acetate underneath, and rub on the caption using type transfers.

At a network station, a computer graphic artist might enter a photo of the flag as a video image onto an electronic paint system. Using the system's special effects, the artist can also create a realistic tear down the center of the flag and make the flag ripple as though blowing in the wind.

High tech or handmade, television graphics make use of a variety of artistic skills: illustration, cartooning, montage, lettering/type design, animation, and computer graphics.

Your job choice is whether to work full time as a staff artist at a network, television station, production house, or a very large private corporate television department.

At television stations and networks, the meat and potatoes of a graphics department is the creation of news story illustrations. In larger stations, there may be separate graphics departments for various shows; in small stations, one graphics department may handle work for all shows, including entertainment and the station's own identification logos and promotional campaigns.

Entertainment programming generally commissions artwork from independent production houses. In these cases, the graphic artists possess a combination of technical wizardry and classic design talent.

In private television, the budgets and scope of productions are usually only large enough for a freelance artist—though animated openings for regular programming sometimes get the full computer graphics treatment via a production company.

TV Graphics Basics

Actual art work can be executed on paper mounted on cardboard, to be shot as a 35-millimeter slide, or on video. Or the artwork may be created directly on video equipment, through computer graphics technology. But, however the artwork is produced, it must meet certain demands of the television medium. What follows is a brief discussion of some of these requirements.

TV Aspect Ratio

Graphics should be designed to fit a horizontal frame with a ratio of 3 to 4, because that is the ratio of the television screen. Otherwise, portions of the graphic may get cut off.

Essential Area

Most television sets are still not flat-screen; they have a rounded frame around the picture tube that cuts off part of the picture. What remains is called the "essential area." While the essential area varies among television brands and models, a safe definition of the essential area is: slightly greater than the central 4/6ths of the total screen area.

Gray Scales

Television does not reproduce the same range of white to black gradations that the human eye can. In fact, television does not reproduce a true black but rather a dark gray. The gray scale is on a ratio of 20 : 1, meaning that the darkest black is only 20 times darker than TV's brightest white. For good reproduction, therefore, television graphics—especially photographs—should have especially strong contrast. Subtle shading doesn't work.

TV Primary Colors

In TV the primary colors are not red, yellow, and blue, but red, blue, and green. The TV medium places special demands on the use of color because certain saturations of colors act "noisy" on camera—meaning that the color vibrates—while others bleach out on camera. You must also take care to use shades that will work on black and white monitors. Two colors—say red and green—of equal hue and brightness, will appear identical on a black and white TV set.

A Day With . . .

News Graphic Artists at an Independent Station

> *This sample day is with the graphic artists of a local independent television station not equipped with high tech graphics equipment. The art department serves a news show that airs at 10 PM every day. The staff consists of one art director and two graphic artists. All art work is produced by hand, and the art director plays a hands-on role as well as a supervisory one. Depending on the day's news, each artist is responsible for as many as 15 to 20 illustrations created from photographs, montages, or drawn by hand. In this example there is a small number of art assignments.*

2 PM

The art director starts the day's work by getting from the news department a preliminary rundown of the news stories for the evening broadcast. The news director has marked on the rundown which stories require illustration. Today's list of stories marked for illustration includes a NASA shuttle delay, the on-going crisis in Lebanon, the stabbing of a nurse from a local hospital, a presidential press conference, and coverage of major league baseball. The list also includes several feature stories for a future broadcast. One such story is on the new trend toward healthy fast food.

Meanwhile, the staff artists come in and file the previous day's artwork for possible re-use should a similar story occur.

3 PM

The art director assigns stories to the graphic artists on the day's shift. For the next two hours, the artists make rough sketches of their illustrations and show them to the art director for approval. The artist working on the story about the stabbed nurse shows a sketch of the medical caduceus symbol—the staff entwined with snakes—a large knife and a violent-looking hand-lettered title: "Fatal Stabbing."

The second artist, assigned to the presidential press conference, takes a stock black and white photograph of the president from the department's photo files. The photo has been used before and has been retouched by hand with pastels so it appears to be in color. The subject of the conference is not yet known, so the suggested caption is simply "Press Conference." The artist proposes using a simple, readable typeface created with letter rub-off transfers. This artist is also working on the fast food story and has several concepts roughed out. One is a complicated surreal illustration in full color showing sushi, snow peas, and other "healthy" food floating on a blue background. The art director rejects it as being too visually complicated, even though it is good art. The art director prefers an illustration of a hamburger and shake with an X over it and a big salad next to it.

The art director choses to handle the sports and NASA illustrations himself. For baseball coverage, the director takes stock photos of the logos of the Yankees and the White Sox. Since they don't know who will win, the illustration will be simple: the two logos side by side separated by the abbreviation "v.s." As for the NASA shuttle delay, a stock photo of the shuttle on the ground is used with the simple caption: "Shuttle Delay."

5 PM

The art director goes to the news department meeting with the producers and news director for the final story line-up. Preliminary sketches of illustrations are approved.

5:20 PM

Since no changes were made to the illustrations, the artists make finished artwork mounted on illustration board.

7 PM

The artists individually bring their finished art to the photo room where it is shot with an ordinary 35-millimeter camera to make color slides. The slides are processed in the dark room.

8:30 PM

The slides are set up in the slide projection machine used for the broadcast. The art director runs them through the projector and checks for spelling, order, and readability. There is still some time—though not much—to correct errors. Sometimes there are spelling mistakes; sometimes a graphic doesn't tell its story well when it is in final slide form and needs to be re-designed and re-executed.

9 PM

The news director or program producer approves the slides.

9:30 PM

The show is ready for taping and broadcast. After the broadcast, the artists go home.

CAREER PATHS FOR THE TELEVISION GRAPHIC ARTIST

This section outlines the basic career paths that exist in television graphics: how to get your first job and gain hands-on graphics experience, what the opportunities are in computer graphics, and notes on future trends.

Low-Tech Graphics

There are two approaches to getting into television graphics. One is to get into television as soon as possible and become familiar with the medium through entry-level jobs. The other is to begin your television news art career outside television. "You're better off getting your first job in any art studio—not TV—because you have to hone your basic skills," advises a network art director/supervisor.

With a portfolio of your print materials, you should, even after only a year's employment, be qualified for a professional-level post in television graphics as a cut-and-paste artist.

First jobs in television graphics for an art student fresh out of school, with little or no professional experience, are generally as production assistants, interns, or researchers for a television station graphics or art department. The smaller stations that have staff artists provide more chance for hands-on experience than large organizations. Corporate television departments may offer more opportunities more quickly. It depends on the size and scope of the department since some use only freelancers.

Intern, Production Assistant, and Other Entry-Level Jobs

See Chapter 2. When applying for these entry-level jobs, be sure to specify your interest in graphics to get assigned directly to the art department. Working in general production is valuable experience also; you can always try to transfer into the graphics department later.

Graphics Researcher

This job is either a low-paying entry-level graphics department position or a nonpaying internship. You will be working directly with graphic designers, filing yesterday's on-air graphics for future use, selecting graphics or graphic elements from the files for today's graphics, ordering slides relating to the day's news stories, checking facts and spellings of names and locations, etc. This position will give you a chance to see how a television graphics department functions from the ground up. You will get a good feel for what designers do, why and how they do it. You will also have a good opportunity to show the art director how you work.

Successful intern/researchers often have a shot at either full-time employment after they graduate from college or at advancement to a junior-level design post. On the minus side, however, you are not likely to have hands-on graphics production work for as long as a year unless you work for a small station or department.

Where to Apply

Send your resume and a cover letter to the art director of local, network, and cable television stations either where you live or somewhere you are willing to live. Follow up your letter with a phone call. Remember, persistence counts.

Cut-and-Paste Artist

Considered an entry-level position at the hands-on graphics production level, a cut-and-paste art job can vary greatly in terms of responsibility depending upon where you work.

At a local or cable station where there is little or no computer or electronic equipment for graphics production, cut-and-paste is virtually the only kind of art work you can do. In fact, you will probably have more graphics assignments at a local or cable news program than you would in network news and will be able to build a portfolio much more quickly.

Both because you produce so much and have to do so in a short period of time, local station graphics positions are terrific proving grounds. You can hone your graphics skills. You learn to think quickly in visual terms that communicate well on television. These positions are excellent launching pads for television graphics careers in news or entertainment.

If you choose to start in a production house or at a network, you will have the advantage of exposure to computer graphics equipment. While your assignments will be cut-and-paste images shot on camera as still art or manipulated by computer graphics equipment, you will be in a position to learn the new technologies. You can learn both by watching what goes on in the department and by getting to know people who can train you. In addition, your employer may send you to training courses to help you master in-house equipment.

Where to Apply

For a cut-and-paste graphics job in cable or local television, write to the station art director, enclosing your resume. In the case of a network, find out if the various programs, including individual news programs (morning, noon, evening, sports, etc.) and various entertainment programs have their own art directors and/or art departments. If so, apply to all of them individually.

In stations of all sizes, contact the public relations or promotion department. They may hire their own artists and designers. Even if the work you land is for print ads or brochures, you will have your foot in the door. Later assignments may be for on-air promotion, and that experience and/or contacts you make at the station can lead to on-air work in news or entertainment.

Management Careers for Low-Tech Artists ————————

While computer graphics appear to be the way of the future, you can remain a traditional artist and still work in television. If you choose to stay in manually-produced graphics (cut-and-paste or hand illustration), you can work for a small nontechnology-oriented local or cable news program. There your career will probably peak at the post of art director, where your responsibilities include attending the news producer's daily meetings, overseeing a small staff of artists, and participating in graphics production yourself.

If you are a "computer-phobe," and choose to work in a network station, your career development is likely to be stunted fairly low on the ladder. Logical vertical moves to supervisory and managerial positions require that you master computer technology, which is fast becoming the industry standard.

High-Tech Graphics:
Becoming an Artist/Engineer ————————

Artists who work with computer graphics equipment are often called artist/engineers and are members of the National Association of Broadcast Employees and Technicians AFL-CIO (NABET), the nationwide union representing most employees at the three major networks and at many local and independent stations.

By considering artists who operate computerized equipment as engineers, NABET has helped artists double their salaries. For example, in 1984 when NABET upgraded artists to engineers at NBC, their salaries jumped from $20,000 to $40,000 overnight. As one network graphics manager says: "TV artists are finally getting a fair shake."

Computer graphics, which are mostly associated with the dramatic program openings that show images swooping and transforming into other images, are also used in daily production. The three major networks all use computers to generate much of their on-air graphics. As prices of electronic equipment come down, more local and cable stations are obtaining it.

The networks take their computer graphics seriously. A special team of artists and engineers, often putting in 20-hour days, spent three years producing the 1984 Olympics graphics for ABC Sports. The spectacular graphics displays included animated diagrams of the 400-meter medley even in swimming. In 1984, NBC used $1.5 million worth of electronic equipment to create the sensational 30-second sequence that opened its reports on the space shuttle Challenger. In this case, rather than animated diagrams, NBC used actual video tape footage of the Challenger, which computer graphics equipment then manipulated in a way that it swooped, flipped, and turned to the rhythms of a specially composed Henry Mancini score.

Artist/Engineer

This position does not necessarily require that you know how to use the computer graphics equipment, although of course experience with it is preferred. The major networks are still learning how to use the new technology, and there is still a willingness to train. "Sometimes we do take artists with print backgrounds, but only if they show strong illustration and design because that can be applied directly to the electronic paint system," says a network art director. "Everything you can do on a drawing board you can now do on the paint system—the stylus gives you access to colors, wash, airbrush, chalk, and line. So, it's still not too late for the conventional artist to take up computer graphics in television—the transition can still be made!"

You can make the transition from print or flat art experience —and some art directors even *prefer* artists with conventional training. One local art director who was looking for an artist with experience using Dubner, the most popular real-time animation equipment brand, complained that many applicants were terrific technically but lacked a good design sense.

One network art director/supervisor sums up the requisite experience for computer graphics positions this way: "You have to have honed your basic design skills first. You can't skip that phase. Remember, sometimes the equipment dies . . . you have to be able to draw a circle, not just rely on an automatic computer-generated one."

Where to Apply

At a large network station, apply directly to the art directors of each news program, including sports and entertainment. At smaller stations and cable, you'll have to call first and find out from the graphics department if it has much or any computer graphics equipment.

Designer/Engineer

A designer/engineer is essentially a senior level artist/engineer with some supervisory responsibility. The main difference is that the designer/engineer is expected to be proficient with the principal types of computer/graphics equipment: paintbox systems, character generators, real-time transform animation, frame stores, and most post-production effects.

A designer/engineer should have two to three years of professional graphics design experience including at least one year of computer graphics hands-on work. In addition, the position may require supervisory experience of both in-house staff and outside graphics services vendors.

Where to Apply

Graphic designer/engineer positions exist in sophisticated graphics departments. Your best bet is to try major networks, very large affiliate stations in major markets, and significant cable news network stations.

Show Lead

A show lead is the next step up from a designer and is a position almost exclusive in a network-sized operation. As its name implies, a show lead is the person in charge of the graphics for a particular show. The show lead's responsibilities include attending the daily production meetings for the show, suggesting concepts for appropriate and requested graphics, and determining the producer's needs. The show lead assigns the graphics to designers and artists; oversees production of the graphics and works closely with both the producer and design staff on any necessary revisions.

Where to Apply

Apply directly to the art director in charge of graphics for a news station. In general, restrict your search to the three major networks and network affiliates in major markets.

Management Careers for High-Tech Artists

The higher level positions in a network graphics department are generally filled from within. Graphic designers with a thorough knowledge of the entire department, its equipment and the news process and those who show evidence of managerial talent are the most likely prospects for promotion. However, superstar technical and artistic wizards can certainly hop from network to network, and do.

While there are no hard and fast rules for getting positions from supervisor through art director, there are a few generalizations that are safe enough to make. An art director at a low-tech small station might be able to land a job as an artist/engineer at a major network. An art director at a relatively sophisticated smaller station with experienced computer graphics equipment may qualify for a show lead position at a network.

A network art director in news or entertainment may be able to move to a production house or an advertising agency. The reverse is also true; a director in a production house or agency can switch to a network or station position, but to do so may have to take a pay cut.

Of the three managerial posts found in a large network department—design, operations, and administration—only the design post is directly related to art skills. A design manager is responsible for special projects such as election news or inaugural coverage or a redesign of the station's logos or new show openings. Such a post would be a job for someone with considerable news experience, preferably in that department.

The other two managers—operations and administration—are primarily engineering and personnel oriented, respectively. Of the two, an artist is more likely to move into the administrative position. The artist would gain invaluable experience scheduling and managing the staff—ideal preparation for becoming an art director.

THE ARTIST/ENGINEER'S BASIC TOOLS ─────

Following are descriptions of some of the basic types of computer graphics equipment used today. While equipment is being modified continually by manufacturers, the high cost of current equipment is likely to keep even "out-of-date" machinery in heavy use.

Electronic paintbox systems enable artists to create illustrations digitally and directly onto videotape. They feature color palettes and color mixing and matching, automatic creation of standard geometric shapes, and the ability to alter or touch-up a video image without starting from scratch. Paintbox systems do not substitute electronics for talent—the artist uses an electronic stylus/pen on a drawing tablet the same way one uses a pen on paper, but they make illustrating easier and faster.

Character generators create lettering for captions and also create free-form images generally used to make logos and station identification spots. In addition to providing the artist with a library of type styles and sizes, the character generator can also manipulate color, provide shadowing, produce a three-dimensional look, reverse type, and other special effects.

Real-time transform animation equipment enables the artist to animate an already-created image on the video "frame." The image can be moved in three ways:

1. The object can be metamorphosed into another shape.
2. The object can be made to spin, flip, or tumble while retaining appropriate perspective.
3. The object's graphic transformations can be accompanied by realistic shading and perspective for a three-dimensional look.

Electronic still stores, electronic libraries for storing video images, enable artists to retrieve quickly and accurately one specific video frame out of thousands.

Post production effects are mega-priced special effects equipment (most common brand names are ADO, Mirage, Kaleidoscope) that creates swooping, flipping, exploding, and other effects. Post effects do not involve illustration and design talent; they are strictly a videotape editing tool requiring a good design eye.

HOW TO GET A JOB

Job Opening: Graphic Designer, TV News: Position available for graphic designer to design and create still and animated news graphics for network news programs using both conventional art and electronic techniques. Design and layout print advertising and produce finished artwork. Operate still cameras for set-up photography work. Produce title animations, storyboards, flat artwork of all kinds. Work with producers and directors under deadline pressure to create animated graphics for news stories.

Requirements: Considerable design experience. Extensive experience producing television news graphics and supervising the work of other designers. Experience working with producers and directors as a "show lead" artist or as an art director for a network affiliate station. Experience in developing and overseeing promotion, advertising, and programming campaigns. Experience operating the Quantel paintbox, switchers, character generators, videotape recorders, electronic still stores, cameras, and digital effects devices. BA or certificate in fine arts, commercial art, TV production, or photography.

—Based on actual network job posting.

What kind of training do you need to become a television graphic artist and where can you get it? What do art directors look for when hiring? What should be in your resume? In your portfolio? You'll find general advice about interviews, resumes, portfolios, and reels in Chapter 2. However, here is advice, based on interviews with professionals, specific to graphic artists.

Training and Education

Although a terrific portfolio is the ultimate selling point, a BFA or Certificate of Fine Arts is generally preferred. Courses in computer graphics are especially valuable as are courses in the fine arts with direct applications for paint-box systems.

There are two professional routes that provide the work experience or training you should have. Some art directors advise you to get early professional experience in a conventional art studio. Their rationale is that working on flat art for advertising and promotional materials will develop your design and conceptual skills.

An alternative route is to get early professional experience as a cut-and-paste artist for a small station. As a member of a very small staff (which may consist of only you) you will hone your design skills and learn about television production. "To be a good art director, you need to know a little bit of everything. At a small station, you'll learn the guts of the business," says a major network's art director.

Another important source of training is provided by the vendor schools sponsored by manufacturers of equipment—in this case, usually computer graphics video equipment. For information, see the list of vendor training schools in the Appendix.

Your Portfolio

Whether you are applying for an entry-level job or a higher level post, you need a portfolio that demonstrates your design talent and skill. There are some basic principles that apply to all portfolios, no matter how simple or sophisticated their execution, whether videotape or flat art.

- *Keep it short.* One network art director says: "I don't have time to look at huge portfolios. Ten pieces are enough, but they should be organized well, with a good beginning and a good end."
- *Concept counts.* The design work you put in your portfolio should show evidence of your ability to think conceptually, symbolically. "I look for a thread through the portfolio that shows the artist's thought process and understanding of graphic design," says an art director of a local news program. If your work is in animation, one network art director suggests you bring a storyboard: "I like to see how the idea progressed."
- *Strong and simple.* Television places special demands on graphic design. Since intricate design does not work in this field, organize your portfolio around pieces that display strength and simplicity.

Your Interview

Your personality is as important as your portfolio. "Television news is not like an ad agency where they want to see your portfolio, not you," one local news art director observes. "In television news, teamwork is important, so I want to see how I'd get along with the person and how that person would fit in with the group."

As important as the ability to work in a team is, your ability to work independently within the team structure is equally important. "I like to ask designers how they developed an idea," says a network art director. "I also like to see them show that they can follow through on a project, that they know the devices to use to get the idea done."

A network art director says: "I always ask people to talk about themselves in the interview, because in this business, communications skills are important. It's very important to know how to ask the right questions, to ask for the proper information to make the story's illustration successful."

Finally, an art director wants to know how much you know about the subject of the programs you are going to be working on. Like a producer or a writer, a graphic artist must have a good general knowledge as well as a specific understanding of a program's subject.

UNIONS

Some stations, particularly the larger stations, both local and network, are union shops. This means you must join whichever union has jurisdiction over your position.

In stations with high-technology graphics departments, artists are usually members of NABET, the National Association of Broadcast Employees and Technicians AFL-CIO. In low-tech stations, if there is a union shop, artists might be members of one of many unions like The Newspaper Guild. The union affiliation may not seem entirely logical at times, but that is because a small group of artists alone cannot constitute a strong and effective union and so join another larger union—even one in a different industry.

Among the advantages of a union membership are job security, higher salaries, paid over-time, extra pay if you work out-of-the ordinary shifts or substitute for a department member who is at a higher pay level.

Among the advantages of a nonunion shop is the opportunity to learn a lot more than just flat graphics. In a union environment, jobs are rigidly defined and union rules dictate who can touch what kind of equipment and perform what kind of task.

In addition to limiting the speed and breadth of your career growth, rigidly defined job descriptions in a union shop can lead to peculiar situations. For example, at one low-tech station in a major market, the art department decided to move to high-tech and ordered a Dubner, a real-time action animation machine. But after it arrived, it lay gathering dust for over a year. The art department belonged to a union that was not the technical union at the station. The latter's rules prevented anyone not in their union from handling technical equipment.

This does not mean that unions are a bad thing. It just means that some rules, originally designed to protect members from management abuses, can interfere with the smooth running of the operation.

FUTURE TRENDS

The industry consensus is that graphics are going to continue wending their computer and electronic ways to more exciting, and they emphasize, useful illustrative capabilities. Supporters of the trend say the increase in technical ability will not mean fewer jobs for artists, but more.

"As the productivity of the artist increases, you simply use more graphics as television transmits more and more information," said Richard Taylor, managing director of Quantel LTD, a leading manufacturer of computer graphics equipment in an article in *Computer Graphics World*: "As the volume of output is increased, more artists will be used because they'll be able to do more things and do them faster."

As a computer graphics manufacturer, Mr. Taylor is not impartial, but his opinion, biased or not, is one that many broadcasting professionals share. Quoted in December, 1980, in *The Wall Street Journal*, Jeff Gralnick, executive producer of ABC-TV's *World News Tonight*, emphasized the important communications benefits of high-tech graphics. "By using supportive graphics, it is possible to convey more information in the limited time we have for news," Mr. Gralnick is quoted as saying. "There are stories we can do now, especially certain economic stories, that we simply couldn't do before we had the graphic techniques to illustrate them."

The real cause of the proliferation of graphics for television news, entertainment, and other programming is economic. Television needs viewers in order to survive. And advertisers who spend a fortune on running their ads are willing to do almost anything to catch the viewers eye, including using special effects and high-tech graphics. Consequently, producers of television programming had to make their programs look as good as the ads that interrupt them. But if anyone is responsible for the rise in television graphics it's the viewer. As one cut-and-paste artist at a low-tech local news station put it: "You have to keep today's viewers amazed. If it doesn't move, it doesn't groove."

A Talk With . . .

Ralph Famiglietta, Jr.
Director, NBC-TV Network News Graphics

> *Ralph Famiglietta is in charge of a team of over 35 designers whose work ranges from cut-and-paste graphics to computer-assisted design and special effects. The department is responsible for all the graphics and animated openings that appear on NBC's network news programs, specials such as those covering national election coverage, and major international news events.*

I started my career in advertising doing pasteups, mechanicals, and layouts. In 1964 I was offered a job in television for a rear-screen projection company. At that time, I didn't even know what television graphics were. I worked on 35-mm slides because that was the era when people used multimedia.

I then left the industry in 1971 and worked as a musician for five years. When I went back into television, it was as a freelance artist. Those were still the days when we used art cards and rear-screen projection. So, I made the transition with television news from cut-and-paste art to state-of-the-art computer graphics. I had to learn a whole new vocabulary: "T-square," "triangle," and "flush-left" were enhanced by "chroma," "phase," "burst," "switcher," "wipes," and "character generators."

What's interesting is that my five years as a musician has turned out to be a real plus. Now that we are creating complex animation openings for NBC News, in addition to the graphics, I occasionally get involved with the music that goes with them.

Design is important but in a production sense it's a very different situation in television news graphics. News graphic artists must understand news, have good organization . . . know engineering terminology and work on extremely tight deadlines.

The most important background is to have production experience in animation, paste-up, mechanical, photoroom, 35-millimeter slides, learning how electronic equipment works, plus the new technology. Independent production houses and small stations provide valuable experience . . . you have a chance to do a lot of different jobs at once, you can really learn the guts of the business! You have to ask questions—you get out as much as you put in. I never hold back. I always ask how things work.

A Talk With . . .

Elan Soltes
Freelance TV Graphic Artist in Hollywood

> *Before becoming an art director and producer of electronic graphics, animation, and special effects, Elan Soltes worked as a writer and producer of video documentaries and specials for PBS, NBC, and HBO. He was a partner in "TVTV," an early groundbreaking video production group, and has worked with Lily Tomlin, Neil Young, Joni Mitchell, and others.*

I got into television graphics indirectly. I had always been very meticulous with the graphics and titles for my own shows, partly as a natural extension of my early work in video where we were trying to create a new visual vocabulary. Five years ago, though, video graphics really didn't amount to much more than a few simple wipes and dissolves, some Chyron, and whatever artwork you could prop up in front of a camera. Then along came the Quantel and the ADO. Suddenly there were black boxes everywhere—Aurora, the Paint Box, Mirage, Bosch, Dubner—and images were flipping, zooming, and tumbling through space. I was able to keep up with the new technology and was called in to help out on a few projects where the producers were having trouble understanding what was possible and how to go about getting what they wanted on the screen.

A lot of my work still involves problem-solving, working with clients to help them get the effects they want without losing track of their budgets. And I find myself getting people out of strange jams. For example, in a commercial spot for a deodorant, the agency wanted the can to glow, but the producers somehow "forgot" until after the spot was shot and edited. So I had to come up with a way to make the can glow after the fact.

I've worked with a wide variety of clients, doing spots for Nissan Motors, music video montages, corporate logos, and title sequences for concert specials, films, and home video entertainment. Lately I've worked with a group of people putting together a syndicated network: helping to develop and create a look, a style—everything from the video logo to bumpers, postcards, even the company letterhead.

I like most of these projects because they tend to be short term, though I do work on a retainer basis with a few clients. I still work on longer-term producing and writing projects, but it can take years from concept to completion. The graphics work helps me fill in the gaps and keeps me from going stir crazy. I have an abiding interest in TV, and this helps me keep up with what's going on. It's rewarding, stimulating, and interesting—and it helps pay the bills, too!

A Talk With . . .

Richard Lee Dickinson
Design Director, WCVB TV-5 Boston

> *TV-5 Boston is an ABC affiliate based in Needham, Massachusetts. As design director, Richard Dickinson's responsibilities go beyond the production of on-air graphics and show openers and range from print promotional materials to interior and corporate design. Dickinson, a graduate of the Rhode Island School of Design, says his entry into television graphics "was not calculated" . . .*

. . . I was looking for a graphic design position and one opened in television. I had been freelancing with different companies, worked full time for an architectural firm in Boston for about a year and then freelanced again and then in 1972 I got a job at this television station as assistant art director.

I oversaw the packaging of news—but not the daily news graphics—did graphics for the station, promotional materials, station IDs, brochures, in-house newsletters, print ads, video ads, show openers, bumpers, and closers.

Working as a designer in television is the same as working as a designer for anything. Design is the communication of ideas visually . . . I don't view television design as so different from any other design position.

I think television is great [for graphic designers] because of the variety of problems and challenges that it poses. I've been at this station for 13 years and in that time I've done five-year plans [for graphics development], booklets, corporate slide shows, annual reports, and prepared and overseen the design of executive offices, prepared major exhibits not only in the station but on location in the New England area. This variety of challenges is what makes it exciting for me.

The down side of television graphics is that a lot of the things prepared for on-air use usually have minus-time, meaning that if you just had a little more time to deal with it, it would be that much better.

Advice

I am a fundamentalist about design. I believe that the discipline of type, shape, form, texture—all those things one learns in school—must be learned to perfection and then applied to television. I would say that knowledge of different types of computers, video, and editing systems is important, but I never put someone's expertise on a certain piece of equipment over their design ability . . . that equipment is changing at too fast a rate.

. . . As for portfolios, to me a portfolio that doesn't have personality is lacking . . . Most of the portfolios I see from the same school, all look like they came from the same person . . . A lot has to do with initiative. A portfolio is a personal "magazine" of information and should entice the reader from beginning to end.

Billy Pittard
Manager of Design, KCBS-TV Los Angeles

> *Billy Pittard, a native of Murfreesboro, Tennessee, has been with CBS owned-and-operated station KCBS-TV since 1984. Eighty percent of the on-air work Billy's department produces is news graphics. His staff of eleven includes seven on-air artists and two print graphic artists who design ads for newspapers and publications such as TV Guide. The department also has a print shop that enables them to produce brochures and other promotional material in-house.*

I got into TV almost by accident. I went to college in my hometown of Murfreesboro, Tennessee, where I was studying advertising and commercial art. I thought I wanted to go to an advertising agency as a creative director or something like that. While I was in school, a classmate friend and I started what amounted to be a small ad agency. In the course of that we both ended up with jobs at a local TV station in Nashville.

The job I got was as temporary assistant to the art director. It was supposed to last for a couple of months. I enjoyed the work so much that I stayed in the business. I worked there for three years as a part-timer doing things like camera cards, tags for commercials, some sales collateral, and basic television and print graphics.

What I liked was the promotional aspect of the work. That's what originally hooked me. A large part of my responsibility was doing movie promos—that's where I learned the basics of television editing and production.

In 1979, a year after I graduated from college, I became art director at the station in Nashville. I continually found new challenges and couldn't get enough of video. It was probably one of the most exciting times in my life—it was full of the thrill of discovery. A lot of what I was able to do was because I enjoyed the technology and didn't know I wasn't supposed to be able to do certain things with the equipment.

Advice

Practical experience is extremely important . . . Once you get your foot in the door and can get your hands on the equipment, you can start to develop your skills and your demo tape.

Remember, a demo tape should not be documentary, it should be fun and entertaining to watch. A good place to start is with a great piece of background music . . . Don't leave lots of black space or tons of color tone bars at the beginning. Make it fun and easy to look at. Package it nicely. Put a nice label on the box. You can create a design for the label that's also used at the beginning and end of the tape. It can make a good impression. It says you take pride in your work and that you know how to present things well.

Be very observant. Study demo tapes from video graphics companies and tape TV commercials and study them to see how they are made. If you ever get a chance to work with someone good, watch carefully, ask questions and then use the first chance you get to try it yourself. Then you'll really be cooking.

9

What Do Television Jobs Pay?

Megabucks are usually associated with salaries in television, and there are indeed healthy salaries and royalties made in network and prime-time production, especially by actors, anchors, and other on-screen "talent" (Table 1). However, the average non-network, behind-the-screen jobs don't come with such glamorous and enviable paychecks.

What follows are several sets of data. Table 2 is an overview of typical pay ranges. Then we show how paychecks vary according to the type of employer (corporate, stations, etc.) (Table 6). Next, we discuss the pay differences according to market size and location of stations (Tables 7 and 8). Finally, we cover future trends in pay.

These figures are not precise. They represent what major unions in the industry quote as salary ranges. There is a great deal of individual variations. In addition to the networks, there are over 1,000 television stations, countless production houses, entertainment studios and public television stations, and pay scales among them are not uniform. The salaries that stations are able to pay depend on many factors, especially market size and market share. Similarly, production companies who have major network and prime-time clients can command top dollar; smaller outfits cannot.

Table 1.   What Do Television Jobs Pay?

News/Anchors-Hosts-Correspondents	Annual Salary
Dan Rather (CBS Evening News)	$2,500,000
David Hartman (ABC's Good Morning America)	$1,900,000
Tom Brokaw (NBC Nightly News)	$1,700,000
Bill Kurtis (WBBM-TV Chicago & CBS)	$1,200,000
Bryant Gumbel (NBC's Today)	$1,100,000
Barbara Walters (ABC's 20/20, specials)	$1,100,000
Walter Cronkite (CBS Special Correspondent)	$1,000,000
Peter Jennings (ABC World News Tonight)	$900,000

Entertainment/Actors	Fee per Episode
Jane Wyman (Falcon Crest)	$105,000
Larry Hagman (Dallas)	$100,000
John Forsythe (Dynasty)	$75,000
Gary Coleman (Diff'rent Strokes)	$72,000
George Peppard (The A-Team)	$65,000
Lee Majors (The Fall Guy)	$65,000
Joan Collins (Dynasty)	$60,000
Linda Evans (Dynasty)	$60,000

Source: News/Anchors-Hosts-Correspondents from "The Daily News," March 20, 1986, Page 93. Entertainment/Actors from "USA Today," April 9, 1985, Page 1–D.

SALARY OVERVIEW

There are several sets of data in this chapter. Table 2, courtesy of the National Association of Broadcasters *1985 Employee Compensation and Fringe Benefits Report,* shows average salaries for a variety of jobs as reported by 426 stations responding to the 1985 NAB survey. Table 3 shows minimum salaries for comparable jobs at a network from a contract with a major union.

Tables 4 and 5 show union rates of pay for directing and writing jobs. As you will see, these union-negotiated rates for prime-time programming (much of which is freelance work) can be substantially higher than network and/or station staff salaries.

Table 2. Median Pay of Television Station Employees

Job	Median Annual Salary	Average Starting Salary
Engineers		
Operator technician	$16,965	$14,798
Maintenance technician	$23,000	$18,354
Operations manager	$38,800	N/A
Chief engineer/director of engineering	$37,310	N/A
Tape/Film Editors		
Tape/film editor	$15,500	$13,536
The Production Crew		
Floor person	$12,810	$12,447
Floor director/stage manager	$18,000	$14,537
Production manager	$26,700	N/A
News photographer/camera operator	$16,371	$14,479
Technical director	$19,000	$16,849
Graphic Artists		
Staff artist	$17,500	$15,304
Art director	$21,200	N/A
Producers/Directors		
Producer/director	$19,486	$16,942
News producer	$21,000	$18,382
Assignment editor	$23,000	$19,184
Program director	$33,500	N/A
Entry-Level		
Secretary	$14,400	$12,158
Production assistant	$13,270	$11,330
Receptionist	$11,253	$9,918
On-Camera Talent		
News anchor	$32,400	$25,445
News reporter	$18,168	$16,014
Sportscaster	$25,100	$20,962
Weathercaster	$28,000	$22,148

Source: 1985 Television Employee Compensation and Fringe Benefits Report, National Association of Broadcasters, Washington, D.C. Copyright 1986.

Table 3. Network Minimum Pay, Based on 1986/1987 Major Union Contract Rates

Job	High-Range Salary	Starting Salary
Engineers		
Studio engineer	$42,900	$24,492
Field engineer	$47,684	$24,492
Construction engineer	$46,202	$24,492
Construction supervisor	$48,464	$29,016
Special service engineer	$48,464	$29,016
Audio/video engineer	$48,464	$29,016
Research and development engineer	$48,464	$29,016
Transmitter engineer	$48,464	$24,492
Maintenance engineer	$48,464	$29,016
Design draftsperson	$46,202	$24,492
Senior design draftsperson	$48,464	$47,684
Tape Editors		
Tape editor	$48,464	$29,016
The Production Crew		
Video camera engineer/operator	$42,900	$24,492
Camera dolly operator	$42,900	$24,492
Light direction engineer	$46,202	$24,492
Video tape engineer/operator	$48,464	$24,492
Video control engineer	$42,900	$24,492
Microphone boom operator	$42,900	$24,492
Sound effect technician	$42,900	$24,492
Audio control engineer	$46,202	$24,492
Staging assistants	$24,778	$17,732
Stage manager	$33,358	$23,556
Senior stage manager	N/A	$43,684
Technical director	N/A	$48,464
Scenic/set designer (United Scenic Artists)	N/A	$47,000
Graphic Artists		
Graphic assistant	N/A	$21,892
Graphic designer	$31,850	$23,244
Graphic design engineer	$48,464	$24,492
Producers		
Writer/producer	$42,900 +	$32,318 +
Writers		
Newswriter	$42,900	$32,318
Entry-Level		
Editorial assistant	$18,772	$17,290
Senior editorial assistant	N/A	$19,734
Desk assistant	$17,498	$13,390

Table 4. Major Union Minimum Fees for Associate Directors, Stage Managers and Directors for Prime-Time Network TV Programs.
(The rates were effective through June 30, 1986.)

	Weekly Studio Rate	Weekly Location Rate
Stage manager	$1,196	$1,671
Associate director	$1,785	$2,499

	Dramatic Show Network Prime-Time		Variety Special Network Prime-Time	
	1/2 Hour	1 Hour	1/2 Hour	1 Hour
Director	$9,964	$16,920	$8,996	$15,107
	7 Days	15 Days	10 Days	18 Days

Table 5. Major Union Fees for Writers and Writer/Producers

News: Network and Major Market Local Program

	Annual Salary High Range Minimum 2 + Years Experience	Annual Salary Low Range Minimum 1 + Year Experience
Newswriter	$41,080	$33,488
	Network Prime-Time 1/2 Hour Program Story + Teleplay	Network Prime-Time 1 Hour Program Story + Teleplay
Writer	$11,651	$17,134
	Day-Time Serial 1/2 Hour Script	Day-Time Serial 1 Hour Script
Script writer	$889	$1,643
	Two-Hour Movie of the Week, Story and Teleplay	
Writer	$34,506	

The most money in behind-the-screen television jobs is predictably in network and prime-time programming, especially prime-time entertainment programming. However, as many professionals have cautioned throughout this book, if you're going into television for the money, don't bother. It takes a lot of patience, luck, and usually many years of very little pay to get there.

Network Minimum Pay

The salaries listed in Table 3 are minimum pay rates only, as negotiated by various unions. The column headed "High-Range Salary" refers to the minimum pay for employees with a certain number of years of experience. To achieve the high range minimum, you generally need no more than five years of experience. While a network may adhere to these minima, in some cases, the pay is much higher such as with producers who have individual contracts.

Overtime work and overtime pay in television is a fact of life. With overtime pay at 50 percent more than straight time, employees generally bring home much bigger paychecks than the salaries here indicate. Overtime can add a good third to your income each year.

Table 5 gives minimum writers fees in a few chosen instances to give you an idea of what kind of payment is possible. Successful entertainment writers command significantly higher prices. These minimum rates are for the period of March 1, 1987, through February 29, 1988.

How Television Pay Varies by Employer Category

Payment also depends on the type of production. The information in Table 6 shows median salary levels among managers and production staff in seven different markets. The job categories covered are Management Staff (president, owner, partner, vice president, general manager, operations manager, government administrator, purchasing agent); Production Staff (production manager, audio-visual director, producer, director, editor); and Technical Staff (chief engineer, engineer, technician).

Table 6.   Pay Variation by Category

	Management	Production	Technical
Teleproduction	$34,700	$28,300	$26,300
TV	$32,700	$27,600	$32,100
Corporate	$40,000	$31,500	$31,800
Medical	$45,050	$25,700	$23,750
Educational	$35,700	$27,200	$25,000
Government	$37,250	$31,300	$32,900
Cable	$30,300	$19,600	$25,600

Source: Video Systems, "1985 Salary Survey," October 1985.

Where the Jobs Are; Where the Best Pay Is ─────────

According to *Video Systems* magazine's 1985 Salary Survey (October 1985), the greatest video activity is in the East/North Central states, which includes New York and its surrounding areas. Accordingly, more video professionals live in the East. The major areas of the United States ranked in descending order of video activity by *Video Systems* are:

1. East/north central states (New York and environs)
2. Pacific states
3. South Atlantic
4. Middle Atlantic

The best pay tends to follow market size of a station or its programming. According to *Broadcast Engineering Magazine's* 1985 Salary Survey, TV managers can expect a 52 percent

Table 7.   How Market Size Affects TV Station Median Salaries

	All Markets	Top 50	Top 100	Below Top 100
Management[1]	$57,750	$69,750	$59,000	$45,950
Engineers[2]	$31,500	$37,500	$28,500	$23,000
Operations[3]	$28,800	$31,800	$24,750	$23,500

Note: (1) Management includes president, owner, partner, vice president, general manager; (2) Engineers includes technical manager, chief engineer, engineer; (3) Operations includes operations manager, station manager, production/program manager.
Source: Broadcast Engineering, "1985 Salary Survey," October 1985.

Table 8.   Salaries for Affiliate and Independent Stations

Category of Workers	Nationwide	Top Ten	51–75	151 +
Affiliates				
Operator/technician	$16,300	$30,700	$17,600	$11,500
Tape/film editor	$13,800	$29,900	$15,100	$10,600
Producer/director	$17,800	$30,500	$18,000	$13,000
News photographer/				
camera operator	$15,200	$33,400	$14,800	$11,400
Production assistant	$12,700	$14,400	$11,100	$11,100
Independents				
Operator/technician	$16,500	$26,700	$10,400	
Tape/film editor	$14,700	$22,400	$10,200	
Producer/director	$21,300	$28,900	$15,300	
News photographer/			Not	
camera operator	$19,000	$31,700	available	
Production assistant	$13,000	$13,200	$11,200	

increase in salary if they move from a below top 100 market station to a top 50 station. Similarly, moving up-market brings an engineer an increase of about 48 percent while operations staff personnel receive an increase of 35 percent (Table 7).

This pattern is confirmed in the National Association of Broadcasters *1983 Television Employee Compensation and Fringe Benefits Report.* Look at this small sampling of median annual salaries for affiliate and independent stations from market to market, and note that some salaries are higher in independent stations rather than affiliates—and vice versa (Table 8).

FUTURE TRENDS

In the past, television salaries have gone in one basic direction: up. However, as the industry matures the seemingly endless pattern of growth appears to have ended. During the research for this book, countless television executives and staff members have said: "The party is over."

Predicting the future is not a precise science. However, we can consider the recent past, some of which is painful. CBS and ABC television networks both cut back on their staffs considerably in 1985 and 1986. Cable News Network did the same a bit earlier.

Of great concern to the networks, and stations in particular, is the fact that television has reached a plateau. The days of constant increases in the number of families with television sets are over. Most families in the United States have television sets. The bigger question is how many more video cassette recorders will they buy to enhance those sets?

The advent of more players in the market has made competition tougher. How much will video cassettes of theatrical movies and original programming divert audiences from viewing scheduled programming? How much audience share has cable taken from the networks and station programming? How much will it? Will a new Nielsen rating method scheduled for use in 1986/1987 show that the networks have less audience share than had been previously estimated? If so, advertising revenues tied to audience share will go down. Unanswered questions like these are behind the reluctance of some employers to hire until the dust has settled and they know what they can afford.

This is not bad news for those who want to work in television. It just means that there may be a period of uncertainty while the industry matures and shakes itself down. Historically the figures have always gone up—salaries, number of employees, opportunities. As the new markets—cable, corporate television and video cassette programming—come into their own, new opportunities will become clearer.

More Pieces of the Pie

The networks stand to lose the most in the shakedown since it is their audience share that is at greatest risk. No one else has as much to lose. This could even turn out to be good news for people in production. After all, the more markets there are for programming, the more programming that will need to be produced.

One sign of increased programming is the recent move by some independent television stations to produce their own situation comedies instead of relying on costly reruns. With popular reruns costing as much as $1 million per episode, independent stations are discovering that it may be more economical to produce their own lower cost programming. They are even exploring developing additional episodes of canceled network shows that had not produced enough programming to go into syndication.

What this means for the people involved in television production is that the future may hold more, but smaller, pieces of the programming pie. That means more production opportunities—not necessarily more money but more room for more people to enjoy making television.

Appendix

Academy of Television Arts and Sciences
4605 Lankershim Boulevard, Suite 800
North Hollywood, CA 91602
(213) 506-7880

Alliance of Motion Picture and Television Producers
14144 Ventura Boulevard
Sherman Oaks, CA 91316
(818) 995-3600

American Electronics Association (AEA)
2680 Hanover Street
Palo Alto, CA 94306
(415) 857-9300

American Film Institute (AFI)
John F. Kennedy Center for the Performing Arts
Washington, DC 90566
(202) 828-4040

American Institute of Graphic Arts (AIGA)
1059 Third Avenue
New York, NY 10021
(212) 752-0813

American Society of TV Cameramen Inc. (ASTVC)
P.O. Box 296
Washington Street
Sparkill, NY 10976
(914) 359-5985

American Women in Radio and Television (AWRT)
1101 Connecticut Avenue NW
Washington, DC 20036
(202) 429-5102

Armed Forces Broadcasters Association (AFBA)
P.O. Box 12013
Arlington, VA 22209
(609) 924-3600

**Association for Educational Communications and
Technology (AECT)**
1126 16th Street NW
Washington, DC 20036
(202) 833-4180

Association of Audio-Visual Technicians (AAVT)
P.O. Box 9716
Denver, CO 80209
(303) 733-3137

Association of Independent Video and Filmmakers (AIVF)
625 Broadway
New York, NY 10012
(212) 473-3400

Association of Media Producers (AMP)
1101 Connecticut Avenue, Suite 700
Washington, DC 20036
(202) 857-1195

**Association of Motion Picture and Television
Producers (AMPTP)**
8480 Beverly Boulevard
Los Angeles, CA 90048
(213) 653-2200

The Audio Engineering Society Inc. (AES)
60 East 42nd Street
New York, NY 10017
(212) 661-8528

Broadcast Designers Association Inc. (BDA)
251 Kearney Street, Suite 602
San Francisco, CA 94108
(415) 788-2324

Broadcast Education Association (BEA)
1771 N Street NW
Washington, DC 20036
(202) 429-5355

Cable Television Information Center (CTIC)
1800 North Kent Street, Suite 1007
Arlington, VA 22209
(703) 528-6846

Corporation for Public Broadcasting (CPB)
1111 16th Street NW
Washington, DC 20036
(202) 293-6160

Direct Broadcast Satellite Association (DBSA)
1800 M Street NW, Suite 400 North
Washington, DC 20036
(202) 822-4297

Electronic Industries Association (EIA)
2001 Eye Street NW
Washington, DC 20006
(202) 457-4900

Federal Communications Commission (FCC)
1919 M Street NW
Washington, DC 20554
(202) 655-4000

Hollywood Radio and Television Society (HRTS)
5315 Laurel Canyon Boulevard
North Hollywood, CA 91607
(213) 769-4313

Independent Television News Association (ITNA)
1414 22nd Street NW
Washington, DC 20037
(202) 872-8700

International Association of Business Communicators (IABC)
870 Market Street, Suite 928
San Francisco, CA 94102
(415) 433-3400

International Association of Independent Producers (IAIP)
P.O. Box 1933
Washington, DC 20013
(202) 638-5595

International Radio and Television Society (IRTS)
420 Lexington Avenue
New York, NY 10170
(212) 867-6650

International Society of Certified Electronics Technicians (ISCET)
2708 West Berry Street
Fort Worth, TX 76109
(817) 921-9101

International Television Association (ITVA)
6311 North O'Connor Road, Suite 110
L.B. 51
Irving, Texas 75039
(214) 869-1112

National Academy of Television Arts and Sciences
110 West 57th Street
New York, NY 10019
(212) 586-8424

National Academy of Video Arts and Sciences
c/o Independent Producers Registry
146 East 49th Street
New York, NY 10017
(212) 486-0471

National Association of Broadcasters (NAB)
1771 N Street NW
Washington, DC 20036
(202) 429-5300

National Association of Educational Broadcasters (NAEB)
1346 Connecticut Avenue NW
Washington, DC 20036

National Association of Government Communicators (NAGC)
P.O. Box 7127
Alexandria, VA 22307
(703) 768-4546

**National Association of Independent TV Producers and
Distributors (NAITPD)**
375 Park Avenue
New York, NY 10022
(212) 751-0600

National Association of Public Television Stations (NAPTS)
1818 N Street NW, Suite 410
Washington, DC 20036
(202) 887-7700

**National Association of Television and Electronic Servicers of
America (NATESA)**
5930 South Pulaski Road
Chicago, IL 60629
(312) 582-6350

**National Association of Television Program
Executives (NATPE)**
P.O. Box 5275
Lancaster, PA 17601
(717) 626-4424

National Audio-Visual Associations (NAVA)
3150 Spring Street
Fairfax, VA 22031
(703) 273-7200

National Cable Television Association (NCTA)
1724 Massachusetts Avenue NW
Washington, DC 20036
(202) 775-3550

National Cable Television Institute (NCTI)
P.O. Box 27277
Denver, CO 80227
(303) 697-4967

National Computer Graphics Association
P.O. Box 3412
Maclean, VA 22103

Public Broadcasting News Producers Association
P.O. Box 14301
Hartford, CT 06106

Radio-Television News Directors Association (RTNDA)
1735 DeSales Street NW
Washington, DC 20036
(202) 737-8657

Satellite Broadcasters Association (SBA)
10 Hancock Drive
Florham Park, NJ 07932
(201) 822-0685

Society of Broadcast Engineers Inc. (SBE)
7002 Graham Road, Suite 118
Indianapolis, IN 46220
(317) 842-0836

Society of Cable Television Engineers (SCTE)
1900 L Street NW, Suite 614
Washington, DC 20036
(202) 293-7841

Society of Motion Picture and Television Engineers (SMPTE)
862 Scarsdale Avenue
Scarsdale, NY 10583
(914) 472-6606

Society of Professional Journalists, Sigma Delta Chi
53 West Jackson Boulevard, Suite 731
Chicago, IL 60604
(312) 922-7424

Society of Women Engineers (SWE)
345 East 47th Street
New York, NY 10017
(212) 644-7855

Television Information Office (TIO)
745 Fifth Avenue
New York, NY 10022
(212) 759-6800

Videotape Production Association (VPA)
236 East 46th Street
New York, NY 10017
(212) 986-0289

Videotex Industry Association
1901 North Fort Meyer Dr., Suite 200
Rosslyn, VA 22209
(703) 522-0883

Women in Cable (WIC)
2033 M Street NW, Suite 703
Washington, DC 20036
(202) 296-7245

Women in Communications (WICI)
P.O. Box 9561
Austin, TX 78766
(512) 345-8922

Women in Film Foundation
6464 Sunset Boulevard, Suite 660
Los Angeles, CA 90028
(213) 463-6040

UNIONS

Broadcast-Television Recording Engineers (BTRE)
3518 Cahuenga Boulevard West, Suite 307
Hollywood, CA 90068
(213) 851-5515

Communications Workers of America (CWA)
1925 K Street NW
Washington, DC 20006
(202) 728-2300

Directors Guild of America Inc. (DGA)
7950 Sunset Boulevard
Hollywood, CA 90046
(213) 656-1220

Film/Video Technicians
6721 Melrose Avenue
Hollywood, CA 90036
(213) 935-1123

Illustrators and Matte Artists of Motion Picture, Television, and Amusement Industries
7715 Sunset Boulevard
Hollywood, CA 90046
(213) 876-2010

International Alliance of Theatrical Stage Employees (IATSE)
1515 Broadway
New York, NY 10036
(212) 730-1770

International Brotherhood of Electrical Workers (IBEW)
1125 15th Street NW
Washington, DC 20005
(202) 833-7110

International Sound, Technicians, Cinetechnicians and Television Engineers
P.O. Box 1726
Studio City, CA 91604
(818) 985-9204

**National Association of Broadcast Employees and Technicians
AFL-CIO (NABET)**
7101 Wisconsin Avenue, Suite 800
Bethesda, MD 20814
(301) 657-8420

The Newspaper Guild (TNG)
1125 15th Street NW
Washington, DC 20005
(202) 296-2990

Producers Guild of America (PGA)
9201 Beverly Boulevard
Los Angeles, CA 90048
(213) 651-0084

Society of Motion Picture and Television Art Directors
14724 Ventura Boulevard
Sherman Oaks, CA 91403
(818) 905-0599

United Scenic Artists (USA)
575 Fifth Avenue
New York, NY 10018
(212) 736-4498
and
3400 Wilshire Boulevard
Los Angeles, CA 90010
(213) 389-6627

Writers Guild of America East (WGAE)
555 West 57th Street
New York, NY 10019
(212) 245-6180

Writers Guild of America West (WGAW)
8955 Beverly Boulevard
Los Angeles, CA 90048
(213) 550-1000

MAJOR VENDOR SCHOOLS

Ampex Corporation
401 Broadway
Redwood City, CA 94063
(415) 367-4161

Studio and portable VTRs, special effects systems, still store and graphics systems.

Chyron Corporation
265 Spagnoli Road
Melville, NY 11747
(516) 249-3018

Graphics and character generators.

CMX Corporation
2230 Martin Avenue
Santa Clara, CA 95050

Editing systems.

Convergence Corporation
1641 McGaw
Irving, CA 92714
(714) 250-1641

Editing systems.

Dubner Computer Systems
158 Linwood Plaza
Fort Lee, NJ 07024
(201) 845-8900

Graphics and animation system.

Grass Valley Group
13024 Bitney Springs Road
Grass Valley, CA 95945
(916) 478-3234

Production and post-production switchers, with digital effects, editing and graphics systems: routing switchers.

Ikegami Electronics, Inc.
37 Brook Avenue
Maywood, NJ 07607
(201) 368-9171

Studio/field camera.

Quantel Inc.
3290 West Baushore Road
Palo Alto, CA 94303
(415) 856-6226

Paintbox and animation editing system. Mirage 3D image
manipulator, cypher-caption generator/image manipulator.
Still stores.

SONY Corporation
1600 Queen Anne Road
Teaneck, NJ 07666
(201) 833-5200

Electronic newsgathering equipment. Studio and portable
videotape recorders and cameras. Editing systems.

Tektronix
P.O. Box 500
M.S. 58-699
Beaverton, OR 97077
(503) 627-1844

Television test, measurement, and monitoring equipment.

BOOKS ——————————————————

Education ——————————————————

Aspen Handbook on the Media, 1979 edition. (New York: Praeger
Special Studies, 1977 3rd ed.), 440 pp.

Includes information on schools.

*The American Film Institute Guide to College Courses in Film and Tele-
vision*, eds. Dennis R. Bohnenkamp and Sam L. Grogg Jr. (Princeton,
NJ: Peterson's Guides, 1980, 7th ed.), 430 pp.

Provides detailed information on schools, their faculty and facilities, listings of courses offered. More than 1,000 institutions are covered.

Broadcast Programs in American Colleges and Universities: 1980–81, (Washington, DC: National Association of Broadcasters, 1981, 15th ed.), 46 pp.

This usually biennial guide lists colleges (2-year, 4-year and graduate programs) by state, showing number of courses and credits offered, major facilities, scholarships or assistantships provided for graduate students, and a list of faculty members.

Internships 1986, ed. Lisa S. Hulse (Cincinnati, OH: Writers Digest Books). $14.95.

Has sections on broadcasting and journalism internships nationwide.

Masters Degree Programs in Instructional Technology, January, 1980, (Washington, DC: Association for Educational Communications and Technology, 1980), 190 pp.

Covers details of 39 programs in the U.S. and abroad.

Overview

Les Brown, *Les Brown's Encyclopedia of Television*, (New York: New York Zoetrope, 1982).

Susan Tyler Eastman and others, *Broadcast Programming: Strategies for Winning Television and Radio Audiences*, (Belmont, CA: Wadsworth, 1981). New edition in preparation.

Bob Shanks, *The Cool Fire: How to Make it in Television*, (New York: W. W. Norton, 1976).

Careers

David W. Berlyn, *Your Future in Television Careers*, 2nd ed. (New York: Richards Rosen Press, 1980).

Jon S. Denny, *Careers in Cable TV*, (New York: Barnes & Noble Books, 1984), pp. 288.

Elmo I. Ellis, *Opportunities in Broadcasting*, 2nd ed. (Skokie, IL: National Textbook Co., 1981).

Lynne Schafer Gross, *The Internship Experience*, (Belmont, CA: Wadsworth, 1981).

Careers in Radio, (Washington, DC: National Association of Broadcasters, 1981).

Careers in Television, (Washington, DC: National Association of Broadcasters, 1981).

Careers in Cable, (National Cable Television Association, 1981), pp. 25.

Production

Ayers, Ralph. *Graphics for Television*, (Englewood Cliffs, NJ: Prentice-Hall, Inc., 1984).

National Association of Broadcasters Engineering Handbook, 6th ed., Bartlett, George, ed. (Washington, DC: National Association of Broadcasters, 1985).

Bretz, Rudy. *Handbook for Producing Educational and Public-Access Programs for Cable Television*, (Educational Technology Publications, 1976), 132 pp.

Breyer, Richard. *Making Television Programs: A Professional Approach*, (Longman, Inc. 1984), 208 pp.

Burrows, Thomas D. and Donald N. Wood. *Television Production: Disciplines and Techniques*, 2nd ed. (Dubuque, IA: Wm. C. Brown, 1982).

Costa, Sylvia Allen. *How to Prepare a Production Budget for Film and Video Tape*, 2nd ed. (TAB Books, 1975), 192 pp.

Davis, Desmond. *The Grammar of Television Production*, (Barrie and Rockliff, 1960), 80 pp.

Elliott, Philip. *The Making of a Television Series*, (Constable, 1972), 180 pp.

Iezzi, Frank. *Understanding Television Production,* (Englewood Cliffs, NJ: Prentice-Hall, Inc., 1984), 158 pp.

Levitan, Eli L. *An Alphabetical Guide to Motion Picture, Television, and Video-Tape Production,* (New York, NY: McGraw-Hill, 1970), 797 pp.

Overman, Michael. *Understanding Sound, Video & Film Recording,* (Blue Ridge Summit, PA: TAB Books, 1977).

Wurtzel, Alan. *Television Production,* 2nd ed. (New York, NY: McGraw-Hill, 1983).

Zettl, Herbert. *Television Production Handbook,* 4th ed. (Belmont, CA: Wadsworth, 1984).

Writing

Blum, Richard A. *Television Writing: From Concept to Contract,* (New York, NY: Hastings House, 1980).

Coopersmith, Jerome. *Professional Writers Teleplay/Screenplay Format Book,* (Writers Guild of America, East, 1983).

Rivers, William L. *The Mass Media: Reporting, Writing, Editing,* (New York, NY: Harper & Row, 1975), 644 pp.

Shanks, Bob. *The Primal Screen: How to Write, Sell and Produce Movies for Television,* (New York, NY: W. W. Norton & Company, 1986).

New and Related Technologies

New Technologies Affecting Radio & Television Broadcasting, (Washington, DC: National Association of Broadcasters, 1981). New edition in preparation.

Tydeman, John and others. *Teletext and Videotex in the United States: Market Potential, Technology, Public Policy Issues,* (New York, NY: McGraw-Hill, 1982).

Videotex Directory: A Guide to the Videotex/Teletext Industries. 1982–83 Ed., (Menlo Park, CA: Institute for the Future, Bethesda, MD: Arlen Communications, 1982).

PERIODICALS

Advertising Age
Crain Communications Inc.
740 North Rush Street
Chicago, IL 60611

Newspaper of the advertising industry. Published twice a week. Job ads, industry trends, programming information.

AIVF Newsletter
Association of Independent Video and Filmmakers
625 Broadway
New York, NY 10012

Monthly. A newsletter for independent film and video artists; includes information on jobs and internships.

American Film
The American Film Institute
The John F. Kennedy Center for the Performing Arts
Washington, DC 20566

Published ten times a year. Covers general articles on commercial motion pictures and home video.

Art Direction Magazine
10 East 39th Street
New York, NY 10016

Monthly. Magazine articles for the graphics professional.

Backstage
Backstage Publications, Inc.
330 West 42nd Street
New York, NY 10036

Weekly entertainment industry newspaper.

Billboard
Billboard Publications, Inc.
One Astor Plaza
1515 Broadway
New York, NY 10036

Weekly news magazine of the music and recording industries. Of interest to those concerned with music television.

BM/E—Broadcast Management Engineering
Broadband Information Services, Inc.
295 Madison Avenue
New York, NY 10017

Monthly magazine about management and engineering for operators and managers in radio, broadcast and cable television.

Broadcast Engineering
Intertec Publishing Corp.
9221 Quivira Road
P.O. Box 12901
Overland Park, KS 66212

Monthly magazine covering broadcast technology news.

Broadcast Week
Titsch Communications, Inc.
2500 Curtis Street, Suite 200
Denver, CO 80205

Weekly business news and features about the broadcasting industry.

Broadcasting
Broadcasting Publications Inc.
1735 DeSales Street NW
Washington, DC 20036

Weekly news magazine of the broadcasting industry.

Cablevision
Titsch Communications, Inc.
2500 Curtis Street, Suite 200
Denver, CO 80205

Weekly news and publication for the cable television industry.

Columbia Journalism Review
700A Journalism Building
Columbia University
New York, NY 10027

Bimonthly.

Computer Pictures Magazine
320 West 42nd Street
New York, NY 10036

Bimonthly for graphic artists.

Daily Variety
Daily Variety Ltd.
1400 North Cahuenga Blvd.
Hollywood, CA 90028

Daily newspaper of the entertainment industry.

DBS News
Phillips Publishing, Inc.
7315 Wisconsin Avenue, Suite 1200 N
Bethesda, MD 20814

Monthly newsletter covering DBS, SMATV, and satellite broadcasting.

The Dial
Public Broadcasting Communications, Inc.
304 West 58th Street
New York, NY 10019

Monthly magazine offering commentaries, feature articles, and schedules for public television and radio stations. Published in fifteen regional editions.

Electronic Media
Crain Communications Inc.
740 North Rush Street
Chicago, IL 60611

Weekly news publication of the electronic media industry.

Electronic News
Fairchild Publications
7 East 12th Street
New York, NY 10003

Weekly newspaper of the electronics industry.

Emmy Magazine
Academy of Television Arts & Sciences
4605 Lankershim Blvd.
North Hollywood, CA 91602

Bimonthly featuring articles about personalities and issues of the
television industry.

Graphics, USA
120 East 56th Street
New York, NY 10022

Monthly. Articles of interest to art directors and graphic artists.

Highlights
National Association of Broadcasters
1771 N Street NW
Washington, DC 20036

Weekly newsletter.

The Hollywood Reporter
Hollywood Reporter Inc.
6715 Sunset Blvd.
Hollywood, CA 90028

Daily newspaper of the entertainment industry.

IATSE Official Bulletin
International Alliance of Theatrical Stage Employees
1515 Broadway
New York, NY 10036

Published quarterly. Covers union news and reports; production
articles; agent listings.

International Television
ITVA
6311 North O'Connor Road, Suite 110
L.B. 51
Irving, TX 75039

Monthly. Private television production and trends.

International Videotex Teletext News
Arlen Communications Inc.
P.O. Box 40871
Washington, DC 20016

Monthly newsletter covering development of the videotex industry, including economics and research.

Journal of Broadcasting
Broadcast Education Association
Department of Communication
205 Derby Hall
154 North Oval Drive
Ohio State University
Columbus, OH 43210

Quarterly journal covering criticism, regulation, effects, and other aspects of radio and television.

Lighting Dimensions
31706 South Coast Highway
South Laguna, CA 92677

Published seven times a year. Forum for lighting directors; occasional job listings.

NAPTE Programmer
National Association of Television Program Executives
310 Madison Avenue, Suite 1207
New York, NY 10017

Monthly publication emphasizing television programming news and trends.

RTNDA Communicator
Radio-Television News Directors Association
1735 DeSales Street NW
Washington, DC 20036

Newsletter of the RTNDA. Emphasizes freedom of information and news broadcasting. Monthly.

Satellite Communications
Cardiff Publishing Co.
6430 South Yosemite Street
Englewood, CA 80111

> Monthly international magazine of satellite news, applications, and technology.

Satellite Week
Television Digest, Inc.
1836 Jefferson Place NW
Washington, DC 20036

> Weekly newsletter concerning satellite communications and related fields.

SMATV Newsletter
Paul Kagan Associates, Inc.
26386 Carmel Rancho Lane
Carmel, CA 93923

> Newsletter published twice monthly. Covers business and regulatory aspects of satellite master antenna television.

SMPTE Journal
Society of Motion Picture and Television Engineers
862 Scarsdale Avenue
Scarsdale, NY 10583

> Monthly technical journal.

Telecommunication Journal
International Telecommunication Union
Place des Nations
CH-1211 Geneve 20
Switzerland

> Monthly.

Television Broadcast Communications
(formerly *Broadcast Communications*)
Globecom Publishing Ltd.
4121 West 83rd Street
Suite 265
Prairie Village, KS 66208

> A monthly covering broadcast technology worldwide.

Television Quarterly
National Academy of Television Arts and Sciences
110 West 57th Street
New York, NY 10019

Journal of the NATAS. Reviews and opinions. Quarterly.

Theatre Crafts
Rodale Press
250 West 57th Street
New York, NY 10017

Published nine times a year. Articles on theater and television design, staging, and production.

TV Guide
Triangle Publications, Inc.
P.O. Box 500
Radnor, PA 19088

Weekly magazine featuring news, feature articles, reviews, and program listings.

TV Technology
Industrial Marketing Advisory Services, Inc.
5827 Columbia Pike, Suite 310
Falls Church, VA 22041

Covers television broadcasting technological and engineering news. Published twice a month.

Variety
Variety, Inc.
154 West 46th Street
New York, NY 10036

Weekly newspaper of the entertainment industry.

Video Systems
P.O. Box 12901
Overland Park, KS 66212

Monthly publication for video professionals.

Video Week
Television Digest, Inc.
1836 Jefferson Place NW
Washington, DC 20036

Weekly newsletter covering program sales and distribution for videocassettes, disc, pay television, and other new media.

Videography
United Business Publications, Inc.
475 Park Avenue South
New York, NY 10016

Monthly magazine featuring articles on video hardware and software. Also features articles on producing and directing in broadcast, cable and private television.

Videonews
Phillips Publishing, Inc.
7315 Wisconsin Avenue, Suite 1200N
Bethesda, MD 20814

Newsletter on management, technology, and regulation in the video industry. Published fortnightly.

Washington Journalism Review
Washington Journalism Review Associates
2233 Wisconsin Avenue NW
Washington, DC 20007

Monthly.

Sources

Chapter 1
Broadcasting Cablecasting Yearbook 1986.
Eastman, Susan Tyler, et al. *Broadcast Programming: Strategies for Winning Television and Radio Audiences,* Belmont, CA: Wadsworth, 1981. (New edition in preparation.)

Chapter 3
Iezzi, Frank. *Understanding Television Production,* Englewood Cliffs, NJ: Prentice-Hall, 1984.
Wurtzel, Alan. *Television Production,* 2d ed. New York: McGraw-Hill, 1983.

Chapter 4
Shanks, Bob. *The Cool Fire: How to Make it in Television,* New York: W. W. Norton, 1976.
Wurtzel, Alan. *Television Production,* 2d ed. New York: McGraw-Hill, 1983.

Chapter 8
Ayers, Ralph. *Graphics for Television,* Englewood Cliffs, NJ: Prentice-Hall, 1984. (in preparation.)

Index